W9-BVU-724

THE BATTLE OF MAJUBA HILL

THE BATTLE
OF MAJUBA HILL

THE FIRST BOER WAR

Oliver Ransford

THOMAS Y. CROWELL COMPANY
New York · Established 1834

TO MY WIFE

First published in the United States of America in 1968

Copyright © 1967 by Oliver Ransford

L.C. Card 68–21370

Printed in Great Britain

CONTENTS

ILLUSTRATIONS

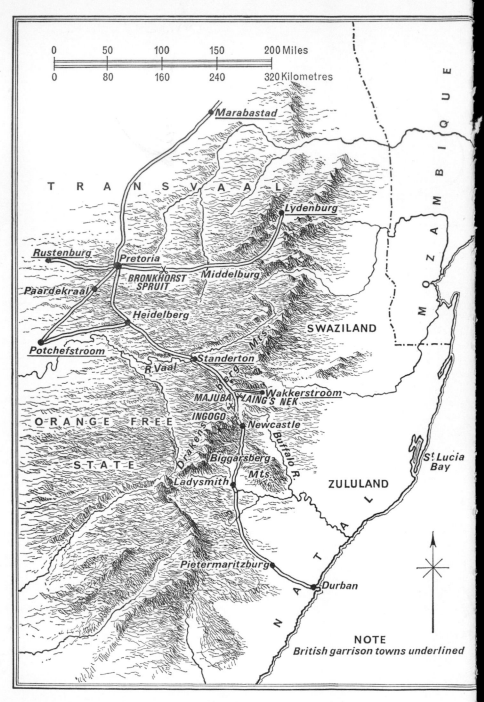

General map

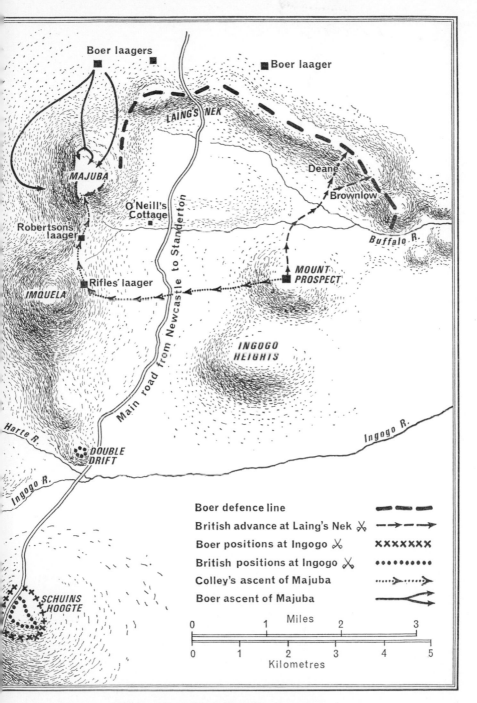

The battles of the Majuba Campaign

ACKNOWLEDGEMENTS

Twice during the last quarter of the nineteenth century Great Britain went to war with the burghers of the Transvaal Republic. The events of the second of these wars, which was fought between 1899 and 1902, have been copiously documented and they are well known to the reading public; those of its 'dress rehearsal' of 1880–81 have been strangely neglected. This book is an attempt to rectify that neglect; but perhaps a better justification for its publication is the fact that the issues which caused the First Anglo-Boer War are still relevant to the political situation of southern Africa today.

My thanks are due to Miss Anna Smith (as well as to two members of her staff, Mrs. Bronstein and Mrs. De Wet) of the Africana Museum, Johannesburg, for courteous assistance and permission to reproduce photographs in her care. Special acknowledgement must also be made to the Air Chief of Staff, Pretoria, who kindly made the aerial view of Majuba Hill available to me. Bulawayo, where this book was written, is singularly fortunate in the calibre of its two librarians, Mr. Stacey and Mr. Johnson, and to both of them I am greatly indebted. For helpful criticisms and advice I also wish to thank Professor F. A. van Jaarsveld of Pretoria, Mr. G. A. Chadwick of Durban, Janie de Kock of Volksrust, Mr. John Gibson, Mr. J. Wakelin, and Mr. John Murray, jnr. The Rhodesian representative of the South African Tourist Corporation went out of his way to provide me with useful topographical information about Majuba Hill, while Mr. G. J. Erasmus, the Town Clerk of Volksrust, made our visits to it especially pleasant and rewarding. Finally I wish to express my thanks to my wife for trudging with me over the battlefields round Laing's Nek, and for encouraging me to write this book. It is fitting that it be dedicated to her.

FOREWORD

'Measured by the numbers engaged, Majuba was little more than a skirmish; judged by its effects, immediate and remote, it almost deserves to be called one of the greatest battles of England.' Such was the opinion of Low and Sanders, the authors of *Political History of England*, and it was not altogether an exaggeration. For although this battle would have scarcely rated more than a couple of lines in the official dispatches of later and bloodier wars, few conflicts can have so decisively affected the history of a subcontinent.

The Battle of Majuba Hill was fought between 365 British soldiers and an almost equal number of Transvaal burghers on a Sunday morning in 1881. By the next day this remote hill in South Africa had become famous throughout the world. For the battle was at once recognised to be the most humiliating defeat ever inflicted on British arms; only later was it identified as the Bunker Hill of Afrikanerdom and the touchstone of an exuberant nation's life. Today, although it was fought less than a long lifetime ago, and its last survivor has only recently died, this battle has already taken on the aura of a legend.

The battle on the summit of Majuba was initiated in an almost haphazard way by an ambitious British General acting against the spirit of his Government's instructions. It cost him his life, and his little army 280 casualties. His Boer adversaries lost only one man killed and five wounded: few victories can have been so cheaply won.

We owe our particular knowledge of the details of this battle to three separate factors. One was the impression their prodigious victory made on the Transvaal burghers, whose paeans of triumph became embalmed in their country's folklore. The second factor was the anxiety of those British officers who survived the disaster to exculpate themselves in writing from any blame or responsibility for it. The third was the

presence on the field of several members of the new profession
of 'special war correspondent' which the telegraph and under-
sea cable had brought into existence; all of them happened to
be particularly gifted reporters; Carter of the *Times of Natal*,
Cameron of the *Standard*, Hay of the *Daily News*, and Aylward
of the *Telegraph*, had led a rush of journalists to the front when
the First Anglo-Boer War broke out, and they wrote vivid on-
the-spot accounts of the action. Other correspondents, like
Melton Prior, Rider Haggard, Lady Florence Dixie, and
Norris-Newman, may have arrived too late to see the fighting,
but they were able to obtain and transmit graphic eyewitness
accounts of it very soon afterwards.

Majuba Hill stands on the border of Natal and the Transvaal.
At the present time its summit is most easily approached
from the small town of Volksrust down the Oliviers Hoek road.
A signposted footpath climbs the north-eastern face of the
hill over a succession of precipitous slopes and broad flat
terraces. This is the way the Boers took in 1881. At the top of
the hill the path opens out on to an extensive uneven plateau
where the engagement took place. This plateau remains almost
exactly as the redcoats and burghers saw it over eighty years
ago; only a small monument and a tiny walled-in cemetery are
new.

Of all the battlefields in the world I judge this one to be the
most compelling. No place is more haunted by its memories.
As one broods there, the present slips very easily into the past;
only a paltry effort of the imagination is required to raise
the mangled soldiers from their graves and set them back in the
places they occupied that Sunday when they died; then the
whole plateau becomes wreathed again in slate-blue smoke, and
the air is filled with the din of battle. The most sentient ears
may even catch an echo of the despairing cry that rose from a
mob of terrified men who finally broke and fled from a horror
they could not comprehend.

The route the British took up this hill of destiny is far more
arduous than the Boer approach; its course lies on the farther
shoulder of Majuba, and you will be told there that it is marked

still by scratches on the rocks left by the soldiers' hob-nailed boots. And such is the evocative spell of Majuba Hill that the modern visitor who follows this same track, does so with the uneasy feeling that the redcoats of 1881 have only just passed by, and he half expects to catch sight of them round every corner.

Part One

PROLOGUE

By 1870, when the Battle of Majuba still lay eleven years away in the future, nearly 80,000 white people—men, women and children—were living in the Transvaal. Though few in number, they and their kinsmen to the south had yet developed a separate language, had formulated their own religious creed, and had come to be like no other community of contemporary European stock. They knew little (and cared less) about the outside world; they had become as much a part of Africa as the Bantu invaders from the north with whom they had contested possession of the southern part of the continent. Although foreigners still spoke of them as 'Boers', a Dutch word meaning 'farmers', these Transvaalers were already beginning to call themselves 'Afrikanders' and 'Afrikaners' to denote their origin. They inhabited a primitive land almost the size of France. All of them shared a deep distrust of the British. Their only wish was to be left alone, free from any interference, free to live exactly as they pleased. And they were very, very tough. For nearly forty years these white men and women had been fighting the half million Africans who lived within the boundaries they had carved out, and they had succeeded in subduing them.

The Transvaalers of those days were nearly all closely related to each other, being descended from the few hundred immigrants of Dutch, German and Huguenot origin who had made their homes at the Cape of Good Hope during the second half of the seventeenth century. Slowly the numbers of these white colonists had grown by natural increase. Many chose to live near the little victualling station set up by the Dutch East India Company which was to become Cape Town, but at least half of the Boers dispersed into the interior, encouraged by the

5

empty pastures waiting for them, and by their own innate aversion to any form of Government control. With the annexation of the Cape by Great Britain at the close of the Napoleonic wars, these semi-nomadic farmers suddenly discovered they had become British subjects. It had been through no wish of their own: an alien Government seemed one shade worse than Dutch authority, and their incentive to escape it increased.

Although these trek-Boers in the hinterland of Cape Colony were only three or four generations removed from the manners and habits of Holland, they had already thrown them off and become espoused instead to their new environment of Africa. They felt happy only in a remote and empty landscape where their own writ might run unchallenged, and where they could watch their herds and flocks filling the veld to its farthest horizons. Any interference with their way of life by Government officials was deeply resented, and they could not abide the British policy of equalisation with the natives. Discontent came to a head in 1834 when slavery was abolished in the Cape without providing adequate compensation for the slave-owners. This blow happened to fall at a time when the grazing grounds of the Cape's eastern province had become impoverished by successive droughts, and when the game on which the Boers depended for their food had been disastrously thinned out. At this time, too, they had become embittered by what was considered to be the very dubious protection offered by the British authorities against marauding natives from beyond the boundaries of the Colony. Accordingly when the restless Boers heard reports of empty fertile grasslands stretching far beyond the Orange River, increasing numbers of them loaded up their goods, gathered their livestock together, quit their farms, and rumbled off in their wagons to make new homes for themselves in the wilds.

These pioneers of the Great Trek marched north at the pace of an ox, but they marched with the faith of evangelists, every mile made shorter because they were convinced they were the Lord's Chosen People and that He Himself was leading them to a new Canaan. Here were the Puritans born again; like them

6

they interpreted their lives in biblical terms, and constantly sought guidance from the Old Testament. By 1838, a thousand wagons were rolling across the high veld beyond the Orange, and some of the more venturesome trekkers were already pressing still farther north across the river Vaal and over the Drakensberg mountains into Natal.

For some time the British authorities at the Cape could not decide how they should regard these 'emigrant farmers'. Had they shed all political allegiance to the Crown when they crossed the Colony's borders? Were they to be allowed to set up independent states in the interior? Should they instead be brought back under British control? These questions were finally resolved by inventing the principle that the trekkers had carried British soil on their boots when they crossed the Orange, and remained British subjects however far they might wander into the wilds. The Crown's authority was in effect reasserted over the trekkers by the Cape Punishment Act of 1836, which applied criminal jurisdiction to all British subjects in southern Africa south of latitude 25°. To the trekkers it seemed then that despite all the perils they had survived, and privations endured, they had still not freed themselves from alien control. Their only resort was to arms. In 1842 they fought British expansion into the republic they had established in Natal—and were driven out of it. Six years later they again took up their guns to defend the independence of the territories immediately beyond the Orange—and were dispersed after a short engagement with British regulars at Boomplaats. All the land between the Orange and Vaal rivers was then annexed by Great Britain under the name of the Orange River Sovereignty. With this development only the Boers beyond the Vaal could claim some degree of independence, and even they except in the extreme north were subject to the Punishment Act.

Then, true to form, British policy in South Africa went into reverse. In 1852, by the Sand River Convention, Whitehall recognised the *de facto* independence of 'the emigrant farmers beyond the Vaal River', and granted them 'the right to manage their own affairs without any interference on the part of the

British Government'. Two years later a further retreat absolved the burghers of the Orange River Sovereignty from allegiance to the Crown, and a second somewhat rickety Boer republic was incontinently established.

It seemed now that the trekkers had gained all they had striven for. They were free to govern themselves, free to negotiate treaties with foreign powers, and free to treat the natives living within their boundaries as they chose. The new Orange Free State settled down to become a prosperous political entity, and during the years ahead showed remarkable progress. By contrast the Transvaalers, the more mettlesome of the trekkers, were plagued by civil disturbances, internal disputes, skirmishes with Bantu neighbours, and even by a highly irrelevant miniature civil war. They were typical frontiersmen living scattered in family groups through their vast country, each settlement almost a law to itself, although owing a loose allegiance to one of the Voortrekker chiefs established at Potchefstroom, Lydenburg, Utrecht, or the Zoutpansberg. These four patriarchs in fact tried to govern four separate squabbling republics. Not until 1856 did they agree to draft a constitution for the whole Transvaal, and were able to establish a united state which bore the auspicious name of 'The South African Republic'.

The new constitution* vested executive power in a President, answerable to a Volksraad which was elected every five years by the burghers of the Republic. One clause in this remarkable document emphasised the fundamental difference in outlook that separated the Transvaalers from the more liberal colonists of the Cape: it read 'The people desire to permit no equality between coloured people and white inhabitants, either in church or state.'[1] It was the enunciation of the principle which a later century would call Apartheid.

*

For nearly twenty years after the Convention signed at Sand River, the burghers of the new republic beyond the Vaal were

* The constitution was finally established in 1858.

8

left to their own devices, which in a political sense meant virtual anarchy. Domestically their way of life followed a characteristic pattern. They preferred to live 'out of sight of their neighbours' smoke' in physical and mental isolation. Their squalid cabins were set up in the veld as far as possible from any road so that the risk of infection to their herds might be reduced. The Transvaal Boers had little contact with the world beyond their borders; they dressed in rough home-made clothes of flannel and corduroy; they wore wide-brimmed felt hats and soft veldskoen on their feet, and they lived off the land. The broad plains around them were black with game; it was cheaper to shoot a buck than to kill one of their own domestic beasts, and in consequence the Boer children grew up to be expert marksmen, who thought nothing of hitting a running buck from the saddle at 400 yards range. Nearly all the burghers' interests were centred round their farm lands and family relationships; the only excitements of the year were provided by regular gatherings at 'Nachtmal', at an occasional mass political meeting to discuss their grievances (for the Transvaalers found their own Government's laws and taxes hardly less distasteful than those imposed by the British), and by infrequent summons to go out 'on commando' to punish some unruly native tribe.

Their isolation would have lasted much longer than it did had it not been for the discovery of diamonds in country contiguous to (and claimed by) both the Transvaal and the Free State. This development in 1867 determined England's return to a more aggressive policy in South Africa. Despite objections from both the Boer republics, the diamond fields were annexed to the Cape, and then, to compound the burghers' irritation, Great Britain proclaimed a protectorate over Basutoland, depriving the Free State of a claim to some fine pasture land. As a final provocation, an outlet to the sea was afterwards denied the trekker republics by Britain's successive seizure of the harbours on the eastern coast-line as far north as Mozambique.

In 1874 Disraeli's second ministry took office, determined

everywhere to advance British imperial interests. During its term control was gained of the Suez Canal, Russian expansion in the Near East was checked, Cyprus was appropriated, the second Afghan War was fought and won, and the title of Empress of India conferred on Queen Victoria. And Whitehall's new forward policy gathered momentum in Africa when Disraeli, on taking office, brought Lord Carnarvon back into the Cabinet as Secretary of State for the Colonies. Although the Earl of Carnarvon was known to his friends as 'Twitters', the name belied him as a politician; he was a determined and far-sighted statesman; only a few years earlier he had presided brilliantly over the federation of the Canadian provinces, and now he was anxious to do something on similar lines for the colonies and republics of South Africa. He spoke eloquently (and with justification) of the economic benefits that would follow confederation, but the timing for his pet scheme was unfortunate. For it soon appeared that neither the prosperous Cape nor Natal had any wish to be saddled with two impecunious republics, while the Orange Free State was still smarting too much from the Basutoland dispute to have any interest in aligning herself with Great Britain. Carnarvon, after these rebuffs, fixed his sights on the Transvaal: he concluded that only by gaining control of that country could he inaugurate his federation; he envisaged the Orange Free State then being brought to heel by economic pressure, and after that it was only a matter of time before the Cape and Natal followed suit. And in 1876, the penurious South African Republic beyond the Vaal seemed to be a fruit ripe for the plucking. The country had been misgoverned for years. The Transvaal pound was worth one shilling. The exchequer was so empty that when State-President Burgers was confronted with a bill requiring the payment of £1,100, he bluntly declared he would rather cut off his right hand than sign, since there was not a penny piece in the treasury to honour it. And the burghers of the Republic, as always, were bitterly divided among themselves on many issues. Some of them had come to detest State-President Burgers for his progressive views; the considerable Dopper community went further and regarded him as a heretic after learning he did not believe the devil possessed a tail, and even accused him of sacrilege when the few golden sovereigns minted during his term of office appeared with his head engraved on them. It was typical of their discord that a fracas convulsed the Volksraad when the well meaning President suggested symbolising the country's unity by adopting a new national flag in place of the old *vierkleur* whose colours were derived from the four original 'republics'. But it was only after Burgers had called out a commando to deal with a rebellious Bapedi chief named Secocoeni, that national morale was seen to have reached its lowest ebb. For when the Boers suffered a sharp defeat, they hastily dispersed without attempting to avenge it. Outside observers were sure that the Transvaalers had lost their old mettle and would never stand up to a determined attack by their African neighbours.

In fact the South African Republic appeared to be hardly viable in 1876. It was surrounded by hostile native tribes itching to invade its territory, and it seemed to have lost the power to repel them. The Zulus presented the greatest threat: their king, Cetewayo, was the nephew of the great Chaka and he had inherited his warlike temper; his impis were mobilised on the country's eastern border and might be unleashed across it at any moment. Reports reaching Lord Carnarvon in London suggested that many, if not a majority, of the Transvaal burghers would welcome annexation to the British Crown rather than face possible annihilation at the hands of the Zulus. He decided to push matters. In the October of 1876 His Lordship dispatched a distinguished pro-consul, Sir Theophilus Shepstone, to Pretoria, the Transvaal capital, ostensibly to report on the situation there, but armed also with discretionary powers to annex the Republic if he was convinced this was desired by most of its white inhabitants. Just before Sir Theophilus sailed, Carnarvon went further: Shepstone's hand was strengthened by secret instructions to proclaim and effect the annexation provided this could be done without bloodshed.[1] This move was not without a precedent; the colony of Natal after all had been acquired for the Crown in a similar sort of way.

It has been suggested that England's sudden solicitude for the Transvaal was inspired by the recent discoveries of payable gold within its boundaries. But it is just as likely that Carnarvon was sincere in his belief that only annexation could prevent a general native rising, and would be the first step in creating the powerful federation of South Africa which he had convinced himself would prove of enormous benefit to all its inhabitants. Yet it must be doubted whether these reasons justified his policy: at the very least it constituted interference in the Transvaal's domestic affairs in gross violation of the Sand River Convention.

In choosing Shepstone to carry out the coup, the Colonial Secretary made a judicious choice. Shepstone was a man of exceptional patience and charm. He was a friend of many of the Boer leaders, and he spoke their language fluently. But there was another side to Shepstone which few people realised at the time: Sir Bartle Frere later came to think of him as the 'Afrikander Talleyrand',[1] and one of his political opponents supported this view when he described Shepstone as 'a crafty-looking and silent man, who never used an unnecessary word or gesture'.[2] The portrait Mr. Aylward drew in fact was of one of those arch-type manipulators, made so familiar to us by the public life of contemporary America.

*

Shepstone arrived in the Transvaal capital early in the January of 1877, escorted by twenty-five mounted policemen and a small secretarial staff which included a young man (who would become better known) named Rider Haggard. He was greeted with enthusiasm by the more credulous of the Pretorians, who laboured under the delusion he had come to liquidate the country's public debt. During the weeks that followed, Shepstone went about Carnarvon's commission with commendable tact and patience. He had been advised to use 'sherry and champagne' methods of diplomacy to sweeten the political climate of the Boer capital, and in consequence his time was divided between lengthy interviews and uncongenial banquets. But every day that passed strengthened his belief that the majority of the Boers favoured a British declaration of annexation. He realised that the Transvaal Government was hopelessly divided, and its officers were too busy caballing against President Burgers to put up much resistance. He saw, too, that the state was bankrupt, since its burghers were still fundamentally opposed to the payment of any taxes. So little cash was available that the State Surveyor was obliged to take his salary in land, while the Postmaster-General found it more convenient to pay himself in stamps.[1] And war seemed imminent with the Zulus; indeed Shepstone was driven to use his personal influence to restrain Cetewayo from taking advantage of the country's weakness. For weeks on end the British envoy surveyed the situation from Pretoria with the cold unblinking eye of a reptile. Then he struck; but even now the business was conducted with discretion. He let it be known that unless the necessary reforms to revive the state's moribund economy were instituted, he could envisage no cure for its malaise but appropriation in the Queen's name. It was a kite flown in the political sky and Shepstone soon saw how the wind was veering. The Transvaal Volksraad met in an uproar to discuss the British envoy's scarcely veiled intentions and, for want of something better, proceeded to censure the State-President for not giving warning of the dangerous situation. The Raad next showed its teeth by appointing Paul Kruger as its Vice-President to emphasise its lack of confidence in Burgers. Then—it wavered, and in a curious mood of repentance adopted some of the constitutional changes which, Burgers had suggested, would retain independence by meeting Shepstone's requirements. After which the Assembly somewhat illogically followed this up by threatening any supporter of the British annexation scheme with punishment for High Treason. It was all very confusing and indecisive; and at the end, all the Raad could agree upon was to close the session by adjourning. Nothing really had been settled.

Shepstone was certain civil war would break out if matters were allowed to drift much further; and he was equally certain now that his secret commission could be effected bloodlessly. He announced to Burgers his intention of annexing the Transvaal Republic in a few days' time, and politely received the President's face-saving protests (whose English wording he had already amiably vetted for him). On the 11th April Shepstone thought it wise to warn Frere, his superior in Cape Town, that a little well-rehearsed opposition could be expected from the Volksraad, whose members feared reprisals and intimidation if they appeared to submit too easily. This should, he insisted, be discounted. 'You need not be disquieted by such action', he assured him, 'because it is a token merely to save appearances and the members of the Government from the violence of the faction. . . . You will better understand this when I tell you privately that the President has from the first fully acquiesced in the necessity for the change and that most of the members of the Government have expressed themselves anxious for it; but none of them have had the courage openly to express their opinions, so I have to act apparently against them.'[1]

Next day, 12th April, 1877, Shepstone formally proclaimed the annexation of the Transvaal, and took over its administration. The state turned out not to be bankrupt after all. Its new ruler found 12s. 6d. in the treasury.

*

For a people so passionately devoted to freedom as the burghers of the Transvaal, there was at first remarkably little reaction to the annexation. The proclamation was accepted with a nonchalance that seemed to justify all Shepstone's expectations. Perhaps the Boers felt stunned by the suddenness of the *fait accompli*; possibly they were too dazed to express themselves. For their part, the state's multifarious creditors and the Britishers resident in the Transvaal, professed themselves delighted with the change; and without doubt the natives living within the country's boundaries were charmed to exchange Boer rule for that of the more liberal English. And all remained quiet for several months; after all, Shepstone's annexation meant security and restoration of credit, and in his proclamation he had promised to set up free representative institutions in the near future. Most of the Afrikaner civil servants even discovered that their consciences allowed them to take the oath of allegiance to the Crown, and they continued in office. The price of land rose, immigrants poured in, and when British troops marched up from Natal, no hostile demonstrations greeted them; they were positively applauded and Pretoria grew to look forward to the concerts given by regimental bands in Church Square.

Naturally a few malcontents pronounced themselves opposed to the new régime, but no one—least of all Shepstone—took much notice of them. Hoping for a more sympathetic hearing in England, a delegation of them headed by Paul Kruger travelled to London to make a formal protest against the annexation. They were very politely received, and shown the sights ('Twitters' butler made a particularly deep impression on the Vice-President). But when they learned the Imperial Government had no intention of restoring independence to their country, Kruger and his companions seemed to accept the rebuff philosophically. They even appeared anxious to assist the new régime, and before the delegates left, Carnarvon was able to write cheerfully: 'They further assured me of their determination to use their best endeavours to induce their fellow-countrymen to accept cheerfully the present state of things, and of their desire, should they be permitted to do so, to serve Her Majesty faithfully in any capacity for which they might be judged eligible.'[1] Nothing could have seemed more encouraging and propitious for the future.

No doubt all would have continued well if Shepstone had fulfilled this original pledge to grant representative government to the Transvaal without delay. But the opportunity of convening the Volksraad while its mood was still accommodating enough to ratify the annexation slipped away as Shepstone became engrossed in his duties as sole administrative authority of the country. And slowly dissident Boer voices, muted before, grew more vociferous. Probably the reaction was inevitable; for one thing the new administration's officers were young, often intolerant, and in Kruger's words 'totally unacquainted with the manners, language, and nature of the Boers'.[1] There were other affronts: the appointment of an Anglican bishop to the see of Pretoria vexed the rigid puritanism of the Doppers; the arming of native auxiliaries by the British alarmed every burgher in the land. Inevitably Shepstone, instead of being regarded as a saviour, came to be accused of having acted in bad faith, and slowly Boer grievances crystallised round the sturdy figure of ex-Vice-President Paul Kruger.

He was a man to whom no one could be indifferent: there were no half tones in him. Norris-Newman, a journalist who came to know the Boer leaders very well, found him 'the most peculiar looking man of the lot';[2] he described him as 'of middle height, with black whiskers and beard, no moustache, thick protruding overhanging nose, high arched eyebrows, very loose black clothes, and a hat thrown far back over his head. He stoops much, is round-shouldered and suffers from a slight defect in speech.' The British heartily disliked Paul Kruger. To them he seemed an ill-favoured and churlish malcontent whose face (set off by its Newgate fringe) appeared grotesquely primeval, and whose mind was filled with sedition and a tremendous obstinacy. His followers, on the other hand, saw him as an ardent patriot, protecting the rights of an oppressed people, and defending the eternal truths. For his part, Kruger had quickly lost the first amiable impression he had formed of the English; he returned their animosity with interest and rallied Boer antagonism to Shepstone's régime. At his prompting, a memorial document protesting against the annexation was circulated through the Transvaal. 6,591 burghers signed it out of a total suffrage of 8,000; only 587 voters resisted intimidation by saying they were in favour of the appropriation.

Criticism of Shepstone's seizure of an independent state was not confined to the Transvaal, nor even to the sympathetic

16

burghers of the neighbouring Free State. The Liberal Conscience in England loudly questioned the right of a great power to coerce a free people; indeed, when the Boers eventually resorted to arms to regain their independence, this section of English opinion openly supported them. For the British have always felt a weakness for the weaker side; what no one suspected at the time was that the Boers in the Transvaal would turn out to be the stronger one.

In 1878, ex-Vice-President Kruger took himself off for a second visit to England, accompanied this time by Commandant-General Joubert, and armed in their document of remonstrance with convincing evidence of the Boer's opposition to the régime. But although he was given more assurances in London about Britain's good intentions regarding the grant of local autonomy, he was also firmly told there was no hope of restoring complete independence. The grim singleness of purpose which marked the remainder of Kruger's life now took root in his mind. He became a passionate opponent of British Imperialism.

The Transvaalers' discontent became more articulate when the conciliatory and easy-mannered Theophilus Shepstone was unaccountably removed from office. He was replaced as Administrator by a very different man—Colonel Sir Owen Lanyon. A more unfortunate choice could scarcely have been made: Lanyon was one of those overbearing military men who possess the unhappy knack of irritating nearly everyone they meet. He stares out from a photograph we have of him with a lugubrious expression in his protuberant eyes; his thinning hair is plastered over a domed pate, and the drooping blimpish moustache makes him seem a very caricature of the Victorian Guards' Officer.

By the time he reached Pretoria tropical service had deeply tanned an already swarthy complexion, and the Boers—always colour conscious—leaped to the unfortunate conclusion that Lanyon was 'nothing but a nigger'.[1]

Colonel Lanyon's flat-footed mental processes did not include the slightest interest in his new subjects. He made no effort to understand their aspirations but proceeded instead to 'endear' himself to them by running their country as though it was a regiment.

The unhappy impression made by Lanyon was softened to some extent by the continued presence in the Transvaal of his superior administrative officer, Sir Bartle Frere, British High Commissioner for South Africa and Governor-General-designate of Carnarvon's proposed Federation. Frere was a 'grave and lofty man', but he did not lack tolerance and understanding. He gauged Boer opposition to the annexation far better than Lanyon, and almost against his will he found himself sympathising with it.

The British Government, however, was less concerned at the time with the rising tide of Afrikaner discontent in the Transvaal than with the task of eradicating native threats to that country's security. More troops were made available to Pretoria; Secocoeni, whom only a few years earlier Burger's commando had failed so signally to subdue, was still at large and closer but before disposing of him the British army turned to deal with the Zulus—and something entirely unexpected occurred: right at the beginning of this 'preventive war' a battalion of British regulars was wiped out by one of Cetewayo's impis at Isandhlwana. Admittedly Lord Chelmsford, the General commanding, was able to retrieve the military situation six months later by winning a belated victory at Ulundi, but the damage to British military prestige had been done. For the first time the Transvaalers saw that the redcoats, after all, were not invincible, and they conceived a fine contempt for their leaders. Moreover they realised that with the removal of the Zulu menace, they had no further need for British protection.

It was ironical that a British victory as well as an earlier defeat had each strengthened the Transvaalers' determination to rid themselves of their alien rulers. But that was how things worked. Yet during 1879 the Boers still hoped to obtain their independence by constitutional means. Frere attended one of their mass protest meetings to discuss their grievances. He

18

realised that in their common detestation of the annexation, the burghers had at last resolved their differences, and were now united as they had never been before. He saw too that unless something was done quickly to conciliate them, they would eventually be driven to armed rebellion. The advice he gave London by the newly opened telegraph cable was to grant the Transvaal a modest degree of self-government without delay.

Unfortunately this wise counsel went unheeded. Frere by this time was out of favour in London. The Government resented the way he had 'lost his sense of subordination' and had provoked a war with the Zulus. Certainly it had not shared his view that only by crushing Cetewayo's military machine could southern Africa escape the consequences of a widespread native rising, and the disaster at Isandhlwana had shown how faulty was Frere's appreciation of the Zulu military strength. Sir Bartle was sharply censured by the British Cabinet; Disraeli even spoke of impeaching him.[1] And presently the High Commissioner was withdrawn to more limited duties as Governor of the Cape. With Sir Bartle Frere's departure went the last chance of settling the Anglo-Transvaal dispute amicably.

In Frere's place, 'England's only general', Sir Garnet Wolseley, was appointed to a High Commissionership for South-East Africa, with plenary powers over both the Transvaal and Natal. Wolseley was a curious mixture of good and bad. Without doubt he was a very competent general; he was also over-confident, and too outspoken for his own good: he had come to be regarded with grave distaste by most of his superiors ever since he embarked on a brave attempt to modernise the British army. Garnet Wolseley in fact was a jaunty, ambitious soldier, blessed with remarkably little tact, and he was every bit as much the martinet as Lanyon. Disraeli once confided to Queen Victoria that Sir Garnet was an 'egotist and a braggart'—but then shrewdly added 'so was Nelson'.[2] That summed up Wolseley very well. People felt about him rather in the way a later generation felt about

Field-Marshal Montgomery—as a difficult, touchy man, but one who on occasions was irreplaceably useful. The agitation in the Transvaal, the Government believed, was one of those occasions. The firm Wolseley touch was just the thing to subdue the discontented Transvaalers, and for some time after the new High Commissioner's arrival it seemed it might. He roared round the troublesome country issuing bombastic proclamations, impressing its people with his Government's obduracy, and discomfiting them with assurances that 'so long as the sun shines the Transvaal will remain British terri-tory',[1] or (in one of the pleasantly varied metaphors which came so easily to him), that 'the Vaal River would flow back-wards through the Drakensberg sooner than the British would be withdrawn from the Transvaal.'[2] But Wolseley was even more remote from Boer opinion than Colonel Lanyon. He forced a new constitution upon the Transvaal which denied its burghers any direct representation, and left their interests in the hands of official nominees. This fell short of even Frere's modest proposals, and the Transvaalers could see that it was really little different than the old autocratic administration of the Cape from which their fathers had escaped in the Great Trek. The malcontents (whom nowadays we would call nationalists) reacted by turning themselves into a militant resistance group led by Kruger and Joubert.

The protests grew shriller, and soon words were replaced by actions. In the December of 1879, a large assembly of burghers at Wonderfontein went so far as to repudiate the Queen's authority, raise the *vierkleur,* and recommend that their defunct Volksraad be convened again to form an alter-native government. Yet there was still no intention of fighting for freedom. As their leaders pointed out, it suited them to wait until the British troops brought in to deal with the Zulus had sailed home again.

And at the beginning of 1880 there was another reason for Kruger to hold his hand. The septuagenarian Mr. Gladstone had recently erupted into a new political campaign. His rich tones went thundering through Midlothian as he denounced the Tory Government for injustices inflicted on innocent people, and they reached across quite clearly to receptive ears in South Africa. For the wickedness of annexing Cyprus and the Transvaal were both important planks of Mr. Gladstone's election platform: he denounced them for inexpediency and dishonesty alike. Speaking at Peebles on 30th March, 1880, the Grand Old Man's indignation rose to a crescendo with a phrase whose fallaciousness must have often come back to mock him after the discovery of the Rand gold-fields: 'I would say this', he cried, 'that if these acquisitions were as valuable as they are valueless, I would repudiate them, because they are obtained by means dishonourable to . . . our country'.[1]

This all sounded most encouraging to the Boers, especially as there seemed little doubt that the vehemence of his oratory would soon sweep Gladstone back into power: and so a deceptive lull lay over the Transvaal as everyone waited for the result of the British general election. The burghers were jubilant when the figures came out. Mr. Gladstone was Prime Minister again.

But Mr. Gladstone in office was a very different person from Mr. Gladstone in opposition. In particular he found it impossible to redeem his election promises regarding the Transvaal without causing grave dissension among his Cabinet ministers, some of whom insisted that the new Government had inherited an obligation to that country's natives which precluded any revocation of the annexation. And so to Kruger's eager enquiry concerning the date when he could be expected to redress the injustices he had so indignantly condemned, the Prime Minister returned a portentous 'Our judgement is that the Queen cannot be advised to relinquish her sovereignty over the Transvaal.'[2] There was no ambiguity about this; even the Boers' most eloquent supporter had deserted their cause: they stood alone; accordingly they prepared for war.

But it still suited them to wait until Wolseley's conceit had practically denuded the Transvaal of troops, before putting things to the touch. By the end of the year only three battalions remained to garrison a country larger than the British Isles.

Presently Wolseley went too, still blustering about his success in overawing the Boers, and assuring everyone that they would never fight. He was replaced as High Commissioner by his friend and protégé Sir George Pomeroy Colley. With his arrival in Pietermaritzburg the cast for the coming drama became complete. For Kruger had already selected his commanders and Lanyon continued to reign in Pretoria, a cranky paper-shuffling fusspot whose vision of the situation was as blurred as ever. He was engrossed at this time with tightening up his plans for more efficient tax-collecting, perfectly unaware that tension in the Transvaal was nearing explosion point.

*

A little time was still left before the shooting started, but that time was running out quickly now. It only needed one small incident to make it run out a great deal faster, and it came in the November of 1880, in the tiny shanty-town of Potchefstroom.

It caught the complacent Colonel Lanyon quite unprepared. He still clung with Wolseley to the delusion that the 'irreconcilables' were bluffing when they talked about fighting a war of liberation. As late as the 25th October, 1880, he had assured General Colley in Pietermaritzburg that he felt no anxiety about the outcome of a mass meeting the Boers had arranged to hold at a farm named Paardekraal the following January.[1] So purblind was he, that on the 7th of November he had depleted his already inadequate number of fighting men by dispatching 285 volunteers to assist the Cape authorities in a campaign against the Basutos. Only when disturbances broke out in Potchefstroom did he wake up to the fact that the ugly situation might be difficult to control with his own resources, and asked Colley to send him up some reinforcements from Natal.

The uproar at Potchefstroom followed a legal action brought by the Government to regain tax arrears of £27 5s. od. from a burgher named Bezuidenhout. The plaintiff was able to prove that only £14 was, in fact, due from him, and while agreeing

Majuba Hill

Sir Owen Lanyon

Sir George Pomeroy Colley

to pay this sum he asked somewhat pertly that it be allowed to stand to the credit of the Republican Government when it came to be reconstituted. The Magistrate retaliated by ordering Bezuidenhout to pay the costs of the action, even though it had been brought against him by the authorities; the costs, he added in his judgement, amounted to £13 5s. 0d., which brought the sum up very tidily to the original amount claimed. Predictably Bezuidenhout refused to pay these costs, and the Court responded by seizing this veld-Hampden's wagon in distraint, announcing that it would be publicly auctioned on 11th November. If the British authorities were being deliberately provocative, they had succeeded very well. One of the more prominent malcontents in the district, Piet Cronje, escorted by a mob of armed horsemen, came pounding into Potchefstroom on the morning of the sale, settled down grimly in its central square, and pulled the Sheriff off the wagon when he put it up for auction. Then, amid triumphant shouts, they restored it to the grateful Bezuidenhout.

This riot seemed just the opportunity to hammer the diehard Boers for which Lanyon had been waiting. He ordered Colonel Bellairs, the officer commanding British troops in the Transvaal, to dispatch a Commandant Raaff and 140 infantrymen down to Potchefstroom to arrest its ringleaders. This as it turned out was far too small a force to overawe Cronje's followers. All it did was to make the excited Boers advance the date of the Paardekraal meeting by one month to the 8th December, 1880, and steel themselves to elect a militant National Assembly which would give approval to armed rebellion.

Belatedly Lanyon realised that he was confronted by something that had grown too big for him. On the day before the burghers were due to assemble at Paardekraal, he so far unbent as to announce that any reasonable requests for representative institutions would be granted to the Transvaal, provided only that the Queen's supremacy was acknowledged. Yet even the calming effect of this proclamation was spoilt by his simultaneous threat to punish all supporters of the rebels. But probably this did not really matter very much: by now the time for talk had passed; the Boers who gathered at Paardekraal were concerned only with action. They appointed a triumvirate of Kruger, Commandant-General Joubert and ex-President Pretorius to act as a provisional government to lead them in the fight for freedom. Then a crowd of 4,000 men and women spontaneously gathered up the stones lying about their meeting place and built them into a great cairn to signify their unity. Finally they planted a *vierkleur* on its summit, and decreed that the Transvaal Republic had been reconstituted.

Even while these events were taking place, Lanyon's crass complacency had returned to him. 'I don't think we shall have to do much more than show that we are ready and sit quiet', he told Colley on the 11th December, since the Boers 'are incapable of any united action, and they are mortal cowards, so anything they may do will be but a spark in the pan.'[1] Events were very soon to refute all these predictions.

Ever since their victory over the Zulu king, Dingaan, on the 16th December, 1837, its anniversary had been kept by the Boers as a day of prayer and national rejoicing. So now it occurred to those assembled at Paardekraal that it would be fitting if their newly-decreed Government was officially proclaimed in writing on that date. The nearest printing press happened to be at Potchefstroom, where Raaff's impotent troops were encamped, and 500 excited burghers galloped to the town on the 15th to arrange for the publication. Next day some of them could not resist riding past the British soldiers stationed there, taunting them with cowardice. It was too much for the English Commander; he ordered a patrol to chase the demonstrators away. A nervous finger pressed a trigger; the firing soon became general, and the soldiers beat a precipitate retreat to the small fort they had built on the outskirts of the town. The First Boer War had begun. People ever since have been arguing about who fired its first shot.

Lanyon was astounded by the news. 'I cannot conceive', he told Colley in bewilderment, 'what can have so suddenly caused the Boers to act as they have.'[2] He would have been even more

24

distressed had he known of the indecent energy with which the Triumvirate now proceeded to wage war. A commando was dispatched to seize the town of Heidelberg which was to be the Republic's provisional and impromptu capital, while others rode off to invest the British forces scattered through the country at Pretoria, Potchefstroom, Lydenburg, Wakkerstroom, Rustenburg, Standerton and Marabastad. But the most important task of all was reserved for a picked commando led by Franz Joubert. His instructions were to intercept a column of British troops under Colonel Anstruther, which spies had reported to be on the way from Lydenburg to reinforce Pretoria, 190 miles distant. There was no time to waste. Lanyon and Colonel Bellairs at Pretoria were known to have been expecting the arrival of Anstruther's relief force ever since the 12th December. Once it came in, they would muster sufficient troops to crush the Boer rebellion at its inception. Everything depended on whether Franz Joubert could dispose of Anstruther's soldiers while they were still on the road. He did so at Bronkhorst Spruit, only thirty-six miles short of Pretoria, on the 20th December. Next day Lanyon received the appalling news that Anstruther's column had been ambushed and annihilated, and that the Boers had begun the war of liberation with a coup that had transformed the entire military situation.

*

There are several aspects of the massacre at Bronkhorst Spruit which are still puzzling. For one thing, although his instructions were to reach Pretoria with the least possible delay, Anstruther seems to have been impelled by no sense of urgency and he took a remarkably long time to get even as far along the road as he did. He received his orders on 27th November, but did not leave Lydenburg for another eight days. The delay was due mainly to his insistence on requisitioning an unnecessarily large number of wagons from unco-operative civilians. Eventually he hired or commandeered thirty, which was far more than regulations allowed; and they slowed down his rate of march disastrously. By 15th December, Anstruther had only got as far as Middelburg, about half way to Pretoria, and even now he did not press his march, but hung about waiting for the rivers ahead to subside, and for repairs to be effected to his wagons. He was well aware that fighting was likely to break out any moment, and on the 17th actually received a message from Bellairs warning him against being ambushed on the road and advising him to 'send forward the natives (voerloopers, etc.) to reconnoitre along the tops of and over the hills before advancing.'[1] Yet even so Anstruther disdained to take the most elementary precautions against surprise.

When Anstruther eventually left Middelburg for the final stage of the march to Pretoria, his force numbered 235 regulars of the 94th Foot (the Connaught Rangers), together with a few medical corps men, and the warrant officers' wives and children who rode in the baggage wagons. The column was strung out for more than a mile along the road.

It was Christmas week, and the men were in a holiday mood. As the scattered column approached a small watercourse named Bronkhorst Spruit, the regimental band in front was absorbed in 'Kiss me mother, kiss your darling daughter', and the dusty soldiers behind accompanied it cheerfully with tuneless voices when they could spare breath from munching the peaches they had bought up cheaply at the last halt.

A little before 1 o'clock on the 20th December, Anstruther, who was mounted, led his column past some scattered farm buildings and orchards to where the road sloped down to the spruit. Suddenly his arm shot up to signal a halt; the band stopped playing, and the singing was replaced by an expectant silence as the soldiers' voices died away.

The Colonel had caught sight of some mounted men halted on a ridge 300 yards ahead, and now, as he turned, more were to be seen in thick cover on both sides of the road. It was Franz Joubert's commando numbering about 200 burghers. (The stricken Anstruther later, however, estimated its strength at 'from 1,200 to 1,500.')[2] Almost immediately a burgher carrying a white flag cantered up to the Colonel and handed him a somewhat equivocal written message. It was signed by the

Triumvirate, and instructed him to halt where he was until
Lanyon had replied to a letter from the provisional Government advising him of the reconstitution of the Transvaal
Republic. The message went on to say that if Anstruther
advanced towards the spruit it would be taken as an act of war;
it gave him two minutes to decide what he would do.

No English soldier could be expected to recognise a junta
that had usurped the Queen's authority; predictably Anstruther
replied that he had orders to march to Pretoria and intended to
carry them out. The emissary then seems to have warned the
Colonel again that his advance would be resisted; and after
exploding with an irritated 'do as you like,'[1] Anstruther
quietened down and asked the horseman to carry his reply to
the Boer commander, and let him know the result.[2] The
messenger nodded his head and rode away. Anstruther said
later that he took this to mean that the Boers would consider
his answer and parley further before taking any offensive action
against him. But almost immediately the burghers began
closing in on the doomed British column, and working round
its rear. Anstruther, suddenly alarmed, shouted to his men to
extend in skirmishing order. But as the bandsmen ran back to
the wagons for their weapons, and the infantry files began to
unsling their rifles and open out, a murderous fire swept
through them. The helpless soldiers were shot down like dogs;
only a few of them were able to return the fire. All the officers
were picked off at once; and within a few minutes 120 dead
and wounded men lay sprawled across the road. Anstruther
himself was hit in several places, and after murmuring that
he 'had better leave a few men to tell the story',[3] ordered his
bugler to sound the 'cease fire'.

The Boers lost only two men killed and five wounded. The
Triumvirate later issued a pompous proclamation to the effect
that the Transvaalers were 'bowed down in the dust before
Almighty God who has thus stood by them, and with the loss
of over a hundred of the enemy, allowed only two of ours to
be killed'.[4] They even described Bronkhorst Spruit as 'a fair
battle'. But of course their 'victory' was ascribed in most

circles, not to the Lord, but to a complete and unprincipled surprise of unsuspecting British soldiers on a wide open road. Indeed it is strange that after presenting their case for independence most correctly and with such exemplary patience for three long years, the Transvaalers should have begun their war of liberation with a massacre that was widely accounted treacherous and dishonourable. It is only fair to say that after the shooting stopped, the burghers behaved very well to the goggle-eyed survivors of the 94th, treating the wounded in makeshift hospitals, and liberating many prisoners on parole. They were particularly concerned to discover that one of the women in the wagons had been wounded. The dead were buried by the side of the road where they had fallen, and legend has it that the peaches in their pockets took root there and grew into a grisly line of fruit trees.

Before Anstruther died of his wounds, he reproached the Boers at Bronkhorst Spruit for committing an unfair act of war, since their emissary had made him believe that no military action would be taken until he had reported to his commander.'[1] Yet in fairness again it must be added that this same emissary swore on oath that Anstruther, before he died, instructed him to tell his General that 'all he did against me was honest'.[2]

Whatever else it did, Bronkhorst Spruit brought an unexpected bitterness into the fighting that followed, and it is the only action in the war which does not redound to the credit of the Boers. It also jolted Lanyon out of his complacency. 'This morning we received very bad news,' he wrote distractedly to Colley. 'I must confess the situation is a most puzzling one, both to me and to everyone who should know the Boer character.'[3] Colley when he heard the news was better able to appreciate its full significance. 'The disaster', he wrote a few days afterwards to his sister, 'has not only been a painful loss to us of many good officers and men, but has changed the whole aspect of affairs—a sort of Isandhlwana on a smaller scale. Had the 94th beaten off their assailants, as I still think they should have done if proper precautions had been taken on the march, the garrison of Pretoria would have been so far reinforced, and the Boers discouraged, that I doubt if Colonel Bellairs would have allowed himself to be invested at all, but think he would probably have taken the field at once and very likely dispersed the Boers.'[1]

The whole British administration in the Transvaal collapsed at once after Bronkhorst Spruit. Over 1,500 soldiers who remained in the country found themselves invested in make-shift forts and had no further influence on the course of the war.* Only General Colley, across the border in Natal, was in a position to retrieve the situation in the foreseeable future, and he would need a good deal of luck to do it. Fortunately for his peace of mind he did not know that from now on tragedy and misery would accompany him during the nine weeks of life remaining to him, or that the troops under his command would suffer the three most humiliating defeats ever known in British military history, culminating in the crowning disaster of Majuba.

* A short account of how the British garrisons fared in the Transvaal during the war is given in Appendix II.

Part Two

THE MAJUBA CAMPAIGN

General Colley and his Boer opponents

The primary responsibility for the British reverses in the First
Boer War rests squarely on the shoulders of Major-General
Sir George Pomeroy-Colley, K.C.S.I., C.B., C.M.G., Her
Majesty's High Commissioner for South-Eastern Africa,
Governor of Natal, and Commander-in-Chief of all British
troops in the Transvaal and Natal.

Sir George was a man of forty-five when the Boer War of
1880 began. The son of the Hon. George Colley of Ferney, Co.
Dublin, he had grown up fortified by the Victorian certainty
that Providence had entrusted the inhabitants of the British
Isles with the task of civilising mankind. At thirteen he entered
the Royal Military College at Sandhurst, and passed out with a
precocious reputation for scholarship. He was already a little
different from the usual run of British subalterns of the time,
and the pattern established by then was to be followed for the
rest of his life. Young Colley was withdrawn and aesthetic; he
painted well and was devoted to Ruskin's works; he even
played the flautina.[1] Indeed some of his contemporaries raised
their eyebrows at the accomplished junior officer, believing
him to be rather more scholarly than it was altogether soldierly
to be. A sketch-book accompanied him everywhere; in it
he would draw scenes that appealed to him or jot down lines of
immature poetry.

At nineteen, when most of his friends were on their way to
the Crimea, Ensign George Colley was posted to South Africa
as a border magistrate. There he saw action for the first time
in the obscure scuffles of a Kaffir War. The frontier districts of
the Cape's Eastern Province were being terrorised at this time
by a native bandit-chief named Tola, and his audacity exerted

a strange fascination on the impressionable young Irishman. At the head of a small column of police, Colley eventually caught up with Tola's gang. Most of them escaped from the skirmish that followed, but Tola, disdaining flight, turned with two sons to face his enemies, shouting: 'Oh, my men, don't run! Follow me.'[1] The memory of those words stayed with Colley for the remainder of his life; curiously enough they might very well have been the ones he himself used twenty-three years later when he watched his own force disintegrate and leave him standing alone on the summit of Majuba Hill.

Lieutenant Colley rejoined his regiment to serve in the China War of 1860, which would by now have been forgotten but for the wanton burning of the Summer Palace at Pekin. Afterwards he entered the Staff College, from which in due course he passed out more brilliantly than any previous student. His exceptional theoretical knowledge soon led to Colley's appointment as an army examiner in military history at Sandhurst, and later he became Professor of Military Administration there. It was a tribute to his quite exceptional professional erudition that, in 1875, he was chosen to write the article on the British army for the ninth edition of the *Encyclopaedia Britannica*.

Then came the Ashanti campaign. During it Colley served under the formidable Garnet Wolseley and found himself responsible for the vital but unheroic task of organising the army transport services when the British pushed up country. From now on Colley was one of Sir Garnet's most favoured protégés, and a prominent member of what military circles irreverently called the 'Wolseley ring'. At the end of the campaign, Colley was promoted full Colonel and made a Companion of the Bath. Everyone regarded him now as one of the army's 'coming men'.

In 1875, when Wolseley was appointed Governor of Natal, he insisted in taking Colonel George Colley out with him as a member of his staff. That same year the Colonel, in the improbable capacity of a Colonial Treasurer, visited the neighbouring Transvaal for the first time; he went to confer with President Burgers on postal and telegraphic matters, but he also carried a confidential mission to test the Boers' attitude to Carnarvon's scheme for federation, and to examine their military strength. The route he took, as his diary tells us, approached the Transvaal by a 'longish hill up from New-castle' and 'some good flat ridges'. He was later to know the 'longish hill' very well—it led to Laing's Nek; and his grave was to be dug on one of the 'good flat ridges'.[1]

1876 found Colley in India, serving as Private Secretary to the Viceroy, Lord Lytton. But three years later when the British Government hustled Wolseley out to Natal again to replace Lord Chelmsford and revenge Isandhlwana, Lytton reluctantly permitted the Colonel to rejoin his old chief.

Colley was a figure of consequence now. In appearance he was a bearded club-man; he had recently been given promotion and a knighthood, and only the year before had married a charming lady fifteen years his junior. But 'that extraordinary run of luck' which, as he had informed his bride in a sort of bemused wonder, 'seems to accompany me in everything, and at times almost frightens me', now appeared to have deserted Sir George Colley. Both he and Sir Garnet arrived just too late to take part in the decisive victory over the Zulus at Ulundi, where Chelmsford restored his military reputation.

Chelmsford's bold gamble in fighting that battle immediately before he was due to be superseded, made an indelible im-pression on Sir George. 'For my own sake', he generously admitted, as Chelmsford withdrew from the African scene with dignity and the laurels of victory, 'I am sorry to have arrived too late for the fun, but I am real glad that Lord Chelms-ford should have had the chance of crying quits with the Zulus.'[2] Nor did it escape his notice that General Evelyn Wood similarly retrieved a defeat at Hlobane with a victory the following day at Kambula. Indeed one suspects, but cannot be certain, that the way these two brother-officers repaired their reputations, lay in Colley's mind when he himself attempted to rectify two military defeats by chancing his 'run of luck' one notch further, and seizing Majuba Hill.

If he had missed the fighting of the Zulu War, Colley at least had plenty of opportunity to study its battlefields on the spot. In the light of the criticisms that were made later of his own dispositions at Majuba, his comments at Isandhlwana make curious reading: 'The more one sees the ground', he gravely notes, 'the more unintelligible the whole affair is—not only that such a force . . . could not make a better stand on ground exceptionally favourable to defence, but also that everybody should have been . . . in entire ignorance of what was taking place in camp, seeing that the whole country is such that half a dozen well posted scouts could have seen everything for twenty miles round.'[1]

His duties as Wolseley's deputy took Colley to the Transvaal for a second time in 1879, and there he met his future opponent, Piet Joubert. Although he was known to be one of the most recalcitrant of the Boers, Joubert impressed Sir George with the sincerity of his feelings. 'There are', Colley wrote later with him in mind, 'a certain number of obstinate, almost fanatical, old Dutchmen, whom one cannot help rather admiring, and who will sacrifice everything, and abandon their farms rather than live under the British flag, or, indeed, under any form of government but their own.'[2]

After peace had been successfully imposed on the Zulus, Colley returned to serve Lord Lytton in India. But within the year, after Wolseley had been appointed to more important duties, Sir George was back in Pietermaritzburg to replace him as supreme civil and military authority in Natal and the Transvaal. He was a Major-General now, and had even hyphenated his name; Sir George Pomeroy-Colley had very nearly reached the top of the Imperial military tree.

His record so far had shown Sir George to be a passionate scholar of the science of war, an extremely capable staff officer, and a devoted lieutenant. If a single theme can be said to have run through his life, it was an admiration, which sometimes almost amounted to hero-worship, for people like Lytton and Wolseley. Perhaps they provided something that was wanting in himself. Until taking up this new appointment in South Africa, there had always been a superior for Colley to lean on, and occasionally he had leaned on them pretty hard. Indeed, Sir George had never really been on his own before, had never held an individual military command, and had no practical experience of the way campaigns depart so frequently from the expected. He was about to learn.

If Colley's ability to command troops in action was still untested, there was no doubt in anybody's mind about his personal charm and integrity. He reminds us a little of General Robert E. Lee, on whom indeed Colley modelled himself, once explaining warmly that Lee 'has always been my greatest military hero, such a mixture of gentleness and everything that was sweet and tender with the grandest military personal qualities'.[1] And there was another side to him which everybody noticed: at a time when bravery was considered to be the most important attribute of a soldier, Sir George combined a curiously refined courage with an almost unmilitary kindliness and sensitivity. From Ashanti a colleague had written of Colley that he was 'never a moment too pre-occupied to bear in mind the needs and rights of others'.[2] And it was this same quality which, in 1880, led the General to appeal repeatedly both to the Boers and to his own men to conduct the Majuba campaign with humanity and charity. In return he expected to find something of his own spirit and purpose in the soldiers he commanded, and frequently he overtaxed them. As General White put it later, Colley had formed 'a dangerously high idea of what a few British soldiers can do'.[3] In the final analysis that was why he failed.

*

When Sir George Colley took up his high position at Pietermaritzburg in 1880 he was plunged at once into a situation of the utmost complexity and peril, but it was some time before he realised it. He can hardly be blamed for this, since Lanyon's dispatches from Pretoria were all couched in reassuring terms calculated to make him underrate the Boers' determination to regain their freedom. It was August before Colley was able to travel north to examine the situation for himself in the Transvaal, and even then he was far more interested in making a 'hurried tour of military inspection'[1] than with considering the burghers' grievances, or with testing their temper. The poor morale of the British garrison troops in the country was his pressing anxiety at the time, while the apparently calm political atmosphere led him to assure his frugal superiors at the Horse Guards that 'in the course of the next two or three months' he hoped to 'effect a further reduction of one regiment in the Transvaal.'[2] Back at Government House in Pietermaritzburg the letters he received from Pretoria during September and October continued to be as unruffled as ever. Lanyon seemed less concerned with Boer restiveness than with his success in collecting taxes, his progress in obtaining recruits for the Basuto campaign, and his own plans for overseas leave. Admittedly, a small note of anxiety crept into the Administrator's communications when he informed his superior of the Potchefstroom disturbances, but the succeeding dispatch was as fatuous as ever. 'The young men seem to think that going on the shoot with soldiers is like going out buck-shooting,' Lanyon wrote early that December, and added: 'I shall be very much surprised if they do anything openly.'[3] Even after open rebellion had broken out, Lanyon was still gullible enough to inform Sir George: 'I do not feel anxious for I know that these people cannot be united, nor can they stay in the field.' But he ended with a casual, 'I presume that you will move up as soon as you hear the news.'[4]

Only on Christmas Day did the blow fall on Colley, and it came as an appalling one. He learned that Anstruther's foot-soldiers had been shot to pieces at Bronkhorst Spruit and that in the Transvaal the Union Jack was only flying in seven impotent and widely separated garrisons. It was clearly time for him to 'move up' if he was to crush the rebellion, and to succeed he would need all the troops he could lay his hands on.

The trouble was that there were so very few of them, for since the end of the Zulu War the British Government had been insisting that the South African garrisons must be reduced. Colley could scrape together scarcely more than a thousand fighting men from the whole of Natal, and he was particularly short of cavalry, as a fine regiment of Dragoon Guards had recently been sent back to India. Across the Transvaal border he knew he would have to face 8,000 armed burghers. Admittedly they were scattered, and furthermore, if his opening moves were successful, he might effect the release of at least some of the 3,000 British soldiers and armed volunteers from the invested garrisons; Bellairs alone commanded nearly 2,000 effectives, and if Colley could raise the siege of Pretoria, it would more than double his own force. What Colley did not yet know was that, in a military sense, Bellairs was moribund and was going to allow himself to be neutralised for the whole course of the war by a much smaller number of Boers.

But Colley had a decision to make, and in making it he was pulled both ways. Should he take the offensive at once? Or should he play for time? A good case could be made for waiting a month or so to allow the reinforcements, which were already on their way from India (the nearest available source) to join him. On the other hand this would risk the rebellion affecting the burghers of the Free State and even spreading to Cape Colony. And delay would undoubtedly jeopardise the safety of the Transvaal garrisons. He was particularly worried about Potchefstroom which was not provisioned to withstand a long siege: its fall would provide the enemy with a considerable propaganda victory, and the thought of the town surrendering to a rabble of farmers while his own force stood waiting intact within striking distance was utterly repugnant to a man like Colley. It was that, more than anything else, the General said later, which inclined him to an immediate offensive.

Yet one cannot help feeling that what really persuaded Colley to invade the Transvaal precipitately was a soldier's instinct to get at the enemy at once, and some queer pent-up vanity to prove himself capable of winning military distinction.

He had felt 'all snug' about his military arrangements before the Bronkhorst Spruit affair, and even afterwards was so hopeful of getting to Standerton, half way to Pretoria, by the end of

January, that he asked Bellairs to prepare a military demonstration there to assist his advance. But the rains were particularly heavy in Natal that year, and the concentration of his troops at Newcastle, thirty miles short of the Transvaal border, took longer than had been anticipated. Colley was exasperated by the delay: the waiting made him nervous and a prey to doubts. On the 17th January we find him still in Newcastle, bleakly wondering what Sir Garnet would be doing in his place. 'I would much like to know', he asked his old mentor like a troubled subaltern, 'whether you at home are blaming my slowness in not moving forward earlier and with a smaller force, or think me rash in attempting to move with so small a one and without waiting for the reinforcements now coming out?' Colley then went on to explain how the local situation looked to him; 'Our weak point, as you will see, is Potchefstroom.' he wrote. 'From all I can gather it might hold out till the middle of February, but not much later, while no important reinforcements can now reach me here till after that date. . . . This it is,' he continues, 'which has determined me to move on without awaiting further reinforcements. I imagine I shall certainly be attacked while crossing the border and probably have a stiff fight at Laing's Nek.'* His plans are further elaborated later in the same letter: 'If I have bad luck,' he goes on, 'I must only hold my own and await the reinforcements; if fair luck, push through to Standerton, and hold on there till the reinforcements arrive; if good luck, push on to Standerton, pick up three more companies there, march on Heidelberg and try to bring them to a decisive battle.'[1]

The little army that was assembling at Newcastle seemed to its anxious commander to be 'as queer a mixture as was ever brought together'.[2] He had succeeded in mustering 1,200 soldiers, and it probably never struck him as absurd that with them he proposed to relieve the 3,000 fighting men in the Transvaal garrisons. His task force consisted of twelve companies of Infantry drawn from three separate units—the

* Colley always spelt it Lang's Nek: the usual spelling has been given in this text, however, for the sake of clarity.

The Boer leaders of the war

Front row, right to left: P. A. Kronje, General N. Smit, Franz Joubert. Piet Joubert is centre in the second row

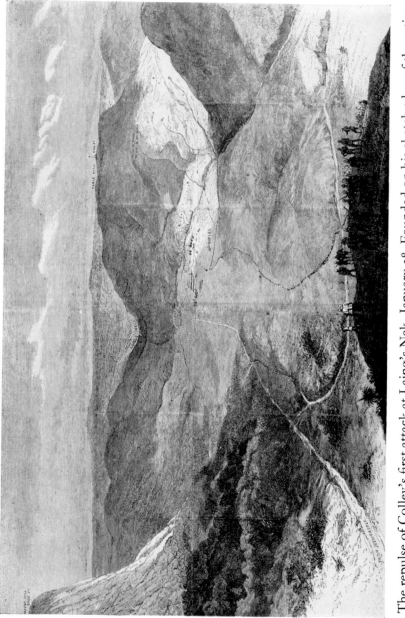

The repulse of Colley's first attack at Laing's Nek, January 28. Founded on his sketch-plan of the action

58th Regiment of Foot (The Northamptons), the 3/60th Rifles (The King's Royal Rifles), and the 2/21st Foot (The Scots Fusiliers). All of them were young, short-service soldiers, lacking stamina, confidence, and *esprit de corps*; and all of them were appallingly bad rifle-shots. They were uniformed in scarlet tunics, blue trousers and white spiked helmets, and were littered with pipe-clayed cross-belts and pouches. In addition to these foot soldiers, Colley had borrowed a contingent of 120 somewhat dazed sailors from men-of-war in Durban harbour to serve in what was grandly termed a Naval Brigade.

He had also found, manned and equipped, two seven-pounder and four nine-pounder cannons. Great things were expected from these guns; the Boers had no artillery at all, and were understood to be extremely apprehensive of shell-fire. In addition the Naval Brigade had been supplied with a battery of rocket tubes. The rockets were fired from copper troughs set up on flimsy bipods, which the Boers rather aptly called 'cow horns'; the troughs gave directional guidance to self-propelled rockets which had a range of over a mile, and their light weight made them useful in mountainous country where conventional artillery could not be used.

The weakest arm of Colley's relief force was its cavalry. On paper he commanded 150 mounted men, but they were only make-believe cavalry. There was admittedly a sprinkling of Dragoon Guards, men left behind for one reason or another when their regiment sailed to India; the remainder were mounted policemen and volunteers from the infantry, scarcely able to sit a horse, let alone fight from one.

The concentration of Colley's soldiers for the invasion of the Transvaal was at last completed by the 23rd January. Two possible routes of advance now lay open to him. One led from Newcastle across country to Wakkerstroom, and although a thrust in this direction might catch the Boers off balance, it would be hindered by bad communications. Colley accordingly rejected it in favour of a direct advance up the main road. It was shorter, but had the disadvantage of passing through difficult hill country, which formed a naturally strong defensive position in the extreme northern corner of Natal.

On the 24th January, 1881, all was ready and General Colley led his small army out of Newcastle to attempt the reconquest of the Transvaal. We can be certain that as he rode up the road towards Laing's Nek, this ardent student of military history was thinking of General Havelock and another scratch force of 1,200 British soldiers which, in rather similar circumstances, had set out from Allahabad twenty-four years before to win glory for its General and regain the Indian Empire for the Crown.

*

The Boers on the other side of the border had meanwhile been leisurely completing their own military dispositions. If Colley commanded an odd army, the one he was going to fight was even odder. Nothing quite like it had ever been engaged by professional soldiers before. As law required, after the declaration of hostilities, the burghers of the Transvaal joined the loose fighting units of their district, called commandos, and divided themselves up into sections under Field-Cornets of their own choice. The Boers provided not only their own rifles but ponies too, and wore their ordinary dun-brown civilian clothes which merged perfectly with the colours of the veld. They looked so unlike soldiers that a shocked Highland officer who fought them in 1881, described an 'ordinary specimen' of a Boer as 'a dirty unkempt-looking fellow, with long hair and beard, very much tanned, his face the colour of mahogany, generally a broad-shouldered, hard-looking man, his dress of all sorts and conditions—usually a coat that will just hold together, and a pair of baggy corduroy trousers. The chances are he has one spur on upside down, his head covered with a broad-brimmed felt hat, high in the crown, and a dirty flannel shirt.'[1] Discipline as known in European armies did not appeal to the Boers. They never considered themselves part of a military machine, but rather as intelligent individuals who were free to move to any part of a battlefield where they considered they would be most useful. They regarded fighting as an unpleasantly dangerous civic duty, and saw no glory in getting themselves killed in it. Indeed, conservation of irreplaceable manpower was part of the strategic creed of these frontiersmen. Although their success at Bronkhorst Spruit had encouraged them, they were frankly apprehensive about the prowess of the regular troops they were going to meet in battle. Yet the Boer's morale was high; they believed their cause was just and their Predikants had repeatedly assured them they were commanded by 'General Jesus'. They were possessed, too, of a remarkable military ability to size up the tactical 'shape' of a terrain, and had great skill in exploiting natural cover. The experience of innumerable native wars, moreover, had taught them an efficient method of storming hill forts, with little loss. Above all, the Boers of 1880–81 were the most accurate marksmen the world had ever known. Although some of them possessed automatic Winchester repeaters, the majority were armed with the Westley-Richards cap rifles which limited their rate of fire; but they took great care never to be caught out in the open, and every shot was made to tell. With some justification the Duke of Cambridge complained after Majuba that his troops in Africa had been defeated by an army of deer-stalkers.

But the Boers' fighting ability was still an unknown quantity when Colley came groping towards them during that rainy January of 1881. Certainly no one in his task force realised that their tactical methods were going to resemble nothing that had been known in war before. What was to make this departure from the orthodox all the more shocking was its invariable success. The burghers did not favour the assault; they preferred to fight on the defensive from behind good cover and in an extended line. It was Colley's misfortune that their poor performance at Boomplaats and their more recent failure against Secocoeni's badly armed tribesmen, had led him to underrate the Boers' fighting quality. But he was by no means alone in his misconception: even their own leaders wondered whether the burghers would stand up to shell-fire, and feared they would disperse at the first check.[1]

41

The Triumvirate's immediate concern after the Paardekraal meeting, as we have seen, had been to immobilise all the available British troops in the Transvaal, and they had succeeded very well. Three thousand men were besieged in improvised forts, scattered across 600 miles of difficult country, and utterly incapable of supporting each other. In the event, since the Boers made no serious effort to assault them, these garrisons, with one exception, were able to hold out without much difficulty until the war ended three months later. (The exception was Potchefstroom which was tricked into surrender by Cronje who withheld news of the armistice negotiations which ended the war.) Once they had neutralised the immediate military threat from these garrisons, the Boer leaders were able to turn their attention to Colley's imminent invasion. Commandant-General Piet Joubert was sent riding down to the Natal border with 2,000 burghers, to establish a standing camp on the banks of the Coldstream. On New Year's Day 1881, he cautiously pushed a patrol across the frontier. But the Triumvirate was still not anxious to proceed to extremes; Lord Kimberley, the new British Colonial Secretary, was already dispatching peace feelers to Pretoria, and there seemed a good chance that the Boers would regain their independence without having to fight for it. But the 23rd January was a date which marked a point of no return; that day, on the eve of leaving Newcastle, Colley addressed an ultimatum to Joubert, ordering him in the Queen's name to disperse his troops. He added an assurance that once this had been done, a statement of Boer grievances would be transmitted to London for the Government's consideration. Joubert replied by moving his horsemen several miles into Natal, and preparing a defensive position on Laing's Nek across the line of the British advance. His troops were hardly dug in before Colley mounted an attack on the Nek, and opened the first of the two curtain-raisers which preceded the sombre drama of Majuba.

No one could have been less like Colley than his adversary, the Boer Commandant-General. Joubert was a tall, burly man of Huguenot extraction, with a determined mouth, fine piercing grey eyes, and an unlikely falsetto voice. He dressed as simply as his men in brown civilian clothes hung about with bandoliers. His face was curiously rectangular: long, black hair was perfectly balanced by a grizzled spade beard, while a heavy black moustache neatly divided the rectangle into two halves. Joubert, in his late forties, was a shrewd self-taught soldier who made war like a professional. His guile and caution had led him to be nicknamed 'slim Piet', but there was a fiery spirit in him too which in a crisis he could be relied upon to communicate to others. He fought the Majuba campaign strengthened by a determination to humble the British (who he firmly believed had been sent by the devil to plague his people) and even more by an intimate knowledge of the surrounding country in which he had lived since childhood.

Joubert was wonderfully well served by his second in command, General Nicholas Smit. Smit was an authentic military prodigy; he possessed originality, a strong taste for fighting, and those high gifts in war of an unfailing practical eye for country, and the ability to exploit every bit of natural advantage in the field. General Butler was not altogether exaggerating when he later summed up this simple farmer-turned-soldier as 'one of the ablest leaders of mounted infantry that have appeared in modern war'.[1] Smit in 1880 was a well-built man half way through his forties; he had a basilisk face and was even more amply bearded than either Colley or Joubert. In him, too, there was a homespun chivalry which shone no less brightly than General Colley's more polished virtues. Colley himself, before he died, paid tribute to this quality: Smit, he said, was 'an intelligent and fine man, courteous and humane in everything connected with the wounded, and gallant in action.'[2]

*

British Reverse at Laing's Nek

Colley's troops trudging up the muddy road from Newcastle through torrential rain made slow progress towards the border, and only approached Laing's Nek on 26th January.

The General had intended to storm the vital heights that same day, but a thick mist came down and forced him to halt four miles south of them at a farm named Mount Prospect. There he threw up protective earthworks and waited for the weather to clear. Next morning the sun burned away the mist sufficiently to let the soldiers scrutinise for the first time the heights which barred the way to the Transvaal.

They saw a high rampart of steep, grassy hills folded together into a ridge fully six miles long which stood defiantly athwart their line of advance. The great ridge was coloured in infinite variations of green and brown; it was high-lighted in places by watery sunshine, and speckled here and there by the moving shadows of clouds racing across the stormy sky. Its crest was bare of trees, but little tongues of brushwood grew from the dark forest at its foot and mounted the ravines which indent the southern face.

There may be scenes more beautiful in the world than the great spur of the Drakensberg Mountains which separates the lush green valleys of Northern Natal from the sterner landscapes of the Transvaal; but when the mood is on them these hills are as lovely as anything Africa can show.

But this day their mood was sombre. The soldiers felt subdued by the great silence and sense of menace which hung over the hills in front of them. It was as though all the themes of South African history had been gathered together there, and were now waiting with concern for Colley's men to make them fall into their appointed places.

From Mount Prospect the ridge was seen to be semicircular in shape, with its two horns running southwards on widely divergent courses, yet enveloping the road leading into the Transvaal. The watching soldiers likened it to a vast amphitheatre set up by nature to overlook a spectacle to be held in the funnel-shaped arena at its feet; and they realised uneasily that they had been cast in the role of its gladiators.

The lowest part of the ridge was situated at its centre and here it took the form of a broad saddle barely 500 feet above the plain. This saddle was the famous Laing's Nek, which took its name from a farmer whose house could be seen standing below the skyline. At first sight the Nek looked like a flaw in the natural defence line of the hills; but the appearance of weakness was deceptive, since Laing's Nek was commanded on either side by formidable heights, and an advance over it could scarcely be made until one flank or the other had been secured.

General Colley stood beside his men staring at the brown-green wall in front of him with a curious avidity and sense of predestination. He felt that this was his ordained testing ground, that these hills had been expecting him to come to them for a long time, that all his training had been but a preparation for the appointment he would keep there.

Through his binoculars Colley could see that the road into the Transvaal wound up to Laing's Nek so gradually that a horse could be cantered up the slope. On either side of the road, however, the ridge rose very much more steeply from the plain. From where he was standing the ground on the left of the Nek was seen to step up 2,000 feet in an abrupt series of ridges and shoulders and grow into the table-topped mountain which the Voortrekkers had called Spitzkop, but which by now had reverted to its African name of Majuba—the hill of the doves.

On the right, the Nek gathered itself rather less sharply into a round-topped ridge which ran south-eastwards for two miles or more before turning away to dip down into the wooded ravines and gullies of the Buffalo River.

And the whole crest of the great ridge in front was alive with Boers, digging trenches and building rough stone schanzes.

After spending some time studying the enemy defences, Colley decided that the least costly way of forcing them would be to storm the Boers' extreme left flank, and then roll up their entrenchments in detail. Unfortunately his sense of urgency allowed him no time to carry out a close reconnaissance of the ground: he was content merely to examine the ridge through his glasses until the clouds came down again, and shut it out of sight.

After days of mist and intermittent rain, the morning of 28th January, 1881 broke bright and clear. A great stir ran through the camp at Mount Prospect. From their vantage points along the ridge the Boers peered down with raw excitement as they watched the redcoats falling in below them. Presently clear bugle calls slanted across the veld from the camp and a long procession of cavalry, infantry, limbered rocket-tubes, and horse-drawn guns wound slowly over the undulating grasslands towards the ridge. It was a breath-taking sight for the burghers; the whole business might have been stage-managed for effect. Five impeccable companies of the 58th and five more of the Rifles were marching towards them, with the bright morning sunlight glinting off their bayonets. Before and behind them rode 150 horsemen, distinctive in blue uniforms. In the rear rumbled the four field guns which their officers had assured Colley, would clear the Nek within fifteen minutes of opening fire. The direction of the soldiers' advance soon pointed towards the Boer left flank resting on the extremity of the domed ridge and on a separate hillock beyond. This sector was held by about eighty burghers that morning, but as soon as Colley's intentions became clear, reinforcements galloped from the Nek to their support.

Only when he had come right up to the foot of the ridge did Colley realise how abruptly it rose from the plain. But he was relieved to see, too, that its very steepness would be tactically advantageous to him, since it screened the men climbing it from the Boers perched along the summit. The upper slopes, however, were commanded by a spur jutting out from the main line of the ridge on the right. Colley realised at once that if he could seize this spur with a quick cavalry attack—and the ascent was gradual enough to permit one—his infantry would be able to scale the slope of the ridge in front of them with comparative immunity. His first objective then must be the spur: the rest would follow. A lull hung over the expectant battlefield as he quietly gave his preliminary orders, and watched them carried out. The plan Colley tied together that morning may be criticised but it was probably as good a one as could have been devised—although everything of course depended on faultless timing.

Unfortunately the timing of the attack that followed turned out to be anything but faultless.

It was nearly 10 o'clock before the troops had been formed up along a start-line below the ridge. An effective rocket bombardment was opened up to pin down the mass of burghers concentrated round the Nek itself, while the field guns, their barrels tilted into extreme elevation, shelled the Boer trenches immediately in front. Only thirty rounds were fired, however, before Colley put in his attack. As the Rifles moved over to the left into a supporting position, the 58th marched up to the base of the ridge and began to climb it. Below them the cavalry commander, Major Brownlow, fretted on the plain, waiting for them to approach the crest. The ascent took much longer than had been anticipated; the slope facing the infantry was so steep that it could hardly be climbed except on hands and knees; indeed the 58th were scarcely half way up the ridge when the impetuous Brownlow gave the order for the cavalry to charge.

Almost immediately things began to go wrong. Brownlow unaccountably veered away to the right of his intended line of advance and galloped up the steepest part of the spur. The horses were badly blown before they had got very far; even so the leading squadron rode right up to the enemy trenches before the men or their horses were shot down. The Boers were badly shaken, and a second hard thrust might well have driven them off the vital spur. But the following squadron, believing their comrades in front had been cut to pieces on the summit, turned at the critical moment and raced back to their starting point, followed by their blaspheming commander who had somehow survived. It was a bad beginning to Colley's first battle, especially as the 58th were by now too far committed to be withdrawn. His own views about the failure of the cavalry were summed up two days later in a letter to Lady Colley: 'There is only one feeling in the camp now', he wrote, 'that had Brownlow's second troop supported him the day was

47

ours. Poor Brownlow, who behaved splendidly, is quite broken-hearted, and when he came down the hill refused to speak to his men or go near them.'¹

Meanwhile the Boers on the spur, having repulsed the horsemen, were free to turn their attention to the infantry clambering up the hill some 400 yards away on their right. They saw a spectacle of pure theatre. For there was a touching quality about this attack of the 58th at Laing's Nek. It was the last assault of the old redcoated army which had served England so long and so well. It was also the last time in history that British regimental colours were carried into battle, and they streamed out in the wind that day as though flaunting the spurious romance of war. The men's parade-ground uniforms caught the morning sun and painted a long sheet of scarlet across the slope. The soldiers were in close order and making very slow progress up the hill; they had no conception of what they would find at the top, but they were as steady as though they were taking part in a field exercise at Aldershot. Ahead of them rode their officers and several members of Colley's staff whom he had permitted to accompany the attack, all mounted and with naked swords in their hands. Far in advance went Colonel Deane, trying to sit erect in his saddle as his charger stumbled and slithered on the muddy slope. The 58th were screened still from the Boers immediately above them on the crest of the ridge, but a dropping fire from both flanks was now causing them a few casualties. The men were breathless as they toiled upwards, and 'teeming from perspiration, which ran into their eyes.'² They had been a little flustered to see the cavalry routed on the right. As they approached the top of the ridge they came to a well-marked brow, beyond which the slope flattened out into a grassy glacis, ascending very gently to the true summit forty yards further on. The Boers had dug their trenches on this crest, sheltered from artillery fire and commanding the glacis. Colonel Deane, still miraculously seated on his charger, arrived first at the brow, and calmly examined the ground that separated him from the enemy. His tactical ideas would scarcely have been considered original by

48

one of Marlborough's officers. He pinned his faith on a shoulder to shoulder advance to within short range of the enemy, followed by meticulous deployment, a volley, and a bayonet charge. So now he ordered the infantry files to open out under cover of the brow; yet before the manoeuvre had been properly completed by the panting men, he called on them to fix bayonets, and they stopped in their tracks. The young soldiers peered across the open ground ahead to where a line of rifle muzzles could be made out on the summit. The moment of crisis hung tautly in the air as they waited for Colonel Deane's next order. Suddenly his sword flashed up in the sunlight and there was a shout of 'charge'. As the men of the 58th hurled themselves across the glacis those below them on the plain heard a long roll of firing. The thing was very quickly over. Their attack simply withered away under the the appalling fusillade. Nearly all the officers were shot at once; Colley's A.D.C. fell shouting *'floreat Etona'*; Deane died far in advance of his men; only one or two redcoats reached the Boer trenches before they were riddled with bullets. To continue the assault was beyond human power. One of the remaining officers gave the order to withdraw; then the survivors on the glacis crawled back to the protection of the brow, and crouched there until they were formed up and marched down the hill again.

There was no panic. Everyone who was present at Laing's Nek that morning remarked on the orderly manner in which the depleted 58th retired. The Boers followed them down the slope, firing from the shoulder, and hoping to turn the withdrawal into a rout, but they were harassed by a burst of accurate shelling. Then the Rifles who were deployed to give supporting fire came into action, and half way down the hill one incredible company of the 58th faced about and checked their pursuers with a volley. But when the battalion reached the foot of the ridge, out of the 480 men who had cimbed it, 150 lay sprawled across its slopes. It was a high figure for any action of such a short duration. How the regimental officers suffered comes out in the account of the battle appearing in the *Mercury* which concluded, 'Sub-Lieutenant Jopp now commands the 58th Regiment'.[1]

General Colley was staggered by the incredible thing that had happened. He was vaguely aware that it had fallen on him to demonstrate the appearance of a new factor on the battlefield—riflemen trained, not to fire in volleys, but to select their own individual targets and to destroy them by accurate marksmanship. But he pulled himself together; disengagement was quickly accomplished, and the soldiers were marched straight back to Mount Prospect.

The Boers lost 14 killed and 27 wounded in the battle of Laing's Nek. They had not suffered in vain. From that morning a fresh spirit, and a gratifying sense of divine favour, wrapped themselves round the Transvaal burghers facing Colley. They had proved themselves in battle, and, as the English General himself admitted, in his official dispatch, had 'fought with great courage and determination';[2] nor had they flinched under shell-fire, but had routed everything that came against them. From now on the Boers were to fight their war of liberation with vastly increased confidence, and certain foreknowledge of victory. And, unknown to themselves, they had begun to create a legend. It would not be an exaggeration to say that the group-awareness of the Afrikaner race, which is so virile today, was born during the Great Trek and then nurtured on the slopes of Laing's Nek overlooking the fair land of Natal.

General Colley (who, one of his officers had already gloomily noted, 'was a great hand at making speeches'),[3] called the British survivors of the action together that evening at Mount Prospect, and told them, in spirit if not in words, that he alone was to blame for the defeat. He went on to promise the 58th that when the time came to renew the assault on the Boer defences, he would see that in recognition of their gallantry they were given the opportunity of sharing the laurels of the coming victory.

Privately he found it very hard to understand what had gone wrong with his attack. How a thin line of Transvaal farmers could have defeated trained soldiers went quite beyond his comprehension. Unfortunately after thinking things over for some time, he reached two conclusions, both of which happened to be wrong and ultimately fatal: he decided that the day of bayonet charges was over, and that troops stationed on the summit of a hill possessed a decisive advantage over those attempting to storm it.

British Defeat at Ingogo

News of the outbreak of rebellion in the Transvaal had been received with mixed feelings in Great Britain. The 'little Englanders' recognised an exquisite opportunity to renew their denunciations of the annexation and to protest against its perpetuation by force of arms, which they declared would be both inglorious and inexpedient. Even the Cabinet was divided in its attitude to the crisis in South Africa. The Prime Minister was himself quite prepared to restore at least quasi-independence to the Boers, and that new year of 1881 he seemed more concerned with stopping the war than with winning it. Indeed Mr. Gladstone became so irritated by Colley's frequently expressed anxiety to whip the rebels before talking peace with them, that he complained to Lord Kimberley, his Colonial Secretary, that 'Colley with a vengeance counts his chickens before they are hatched,' and added, 'his line is singularly wide of ours'.[1] But the feelings of some of his colleagues in the Government had hardened against the Boers after Bronkhorst Spruit, and they argued that for the sake of prestige the Queen's authority should be reasserted in the Transvaal before any magnanimous concessions were made to rebels in arms. In short they wanted Colley to give them a victory, and allow peace to be negotiated from a position of strength.

It was symptomatic of the Cabinet's dissension that, while substantial reinforcements were ordered out to South Africa, Lord Kimberley at the same time dispatched another peace feeler to the Boers, and General Sir Evelyn Wood was appointed to be second-in-command of the troops in Natal.

For Wood was considered to be a man of balance and moderation who was uncommitted to the war party. Kimberley had confidence in his ability to 'play it cool'—more confidence certainly than he had in Colley's. Before Wood sailed, the Colonial Secretary, in an interview, gave him 'to understand he already accepted in principle' the revocation of the annexation,[1] and even disclosed to him his own master plan of partitioning the Transvaal, which he hoped would allow a compromise peace to be made. Kimberley further made it clear that he expected Sir Evelyn not only to relieve Colley of at least some of his military duties, but to curb his pugnacity as well.

The Colonial Secretary's first peace feeler had taken the form of a telegram which he sent to President Brand of the Orange Free State on 10th January, 1881, the same day that Sir George (quite unaware of this development) said good-bye to Lady Colley, and rode out of Pietermaritzburg to join his troops at Newcastle. In this telegram Kimberley asked Brand to act as a mediator between London and Pretoria, and to inform Kruger that Her Majesty's Government did 'not despair of making a satisfactory arrangement' with the rebels provided they desisted 'from their armed opposition to the Queen's authority.'[2] Brand was more than prepared to be helpful, but the insistence on the Boers' 'cessation of armed operations' before the British would treat with them, was to hamper his efforts again and again during the next six weeks. For the demand was, of course, unacceptable to the rebels especially after they had begun to experience military success: this was the rock on which the negotiations repeatedly foundered. But at least Kimberley's overture was more conciliatory than any that had gone before, and for the next two weeks Whitehall, Cape Town, Heidelberg and Bloemfontein bombarded each other with telegrams in their search for a formula acceptable to everyone.

When news of Colley's defeat at Laing's Nek reached London, however, Gladstone's Government subsided into pained silence, and the telegraph line to South Africa temporarily went mute.

Most of the peacemakers' telegrams and cables had been copied to Colley as a matter of course, and most of them had infuriated him. Not only did he disapprove of the Ministry's inclination to negotiate with the Transvaalers instead of defeating them, but after his defeat he now had a personal stake in revenging Laing's Nek before hostilities ended. And so he went ahead with new plans for a break-through into the Transvaal as soon as he had been sufficiently reinforced by troops already on the way from Durban. That first week in February he was very concerned about the safety of these troops coming up the road: his communications were dangerously vulnerable to commandos infiltrating through the foothills of the Drakensberg, and there was some evidence too that the rebels were using Free State territory to threaten the road where it crossed the Biggarsberg. He telegraphed a sharp enquiry to President Brand about this suspected infringement of the Free State's neutrality, and was answered with a firm refutal. But Brand's reply also indicated that he welcomed the opportunity of establishing personal contact with General Colley, the man on the spot; and an eloquent appeal for a truce even wrung a reluctant agreement from Sir George that he would make no further military advance while Brand's efforts for peace were in progress. It was a concession that Colley very soon regretted: Kimberley snubbed him for it with an intimation that any further negotiations with the Boers must be reserved for the British Government, and anyway the General realised that it had tied his hands strategically. In the end, after thinking it over for six days, Colley wired again to Brand that after all he could not 'allow any communication with the Boers to affect his military operations'.[1]

It is difficult, in any case, to believe that Sir George's first protestations of peaceful intentions had been entirely sincere, for on the same day he gave them to Brand, he wrote in a very different spirit to Sir Evelyn Wood who was soon due to land in Durban with more troops. This letter was full of Colley's plans for renewing the attack on Joubert. He intended, he told Wood, to add two infantry battalions and one cavalry regiment to his field force at Mount Prospect; as for General Wood, he was to take command of a second column of three battalions based in Newcastle, with which he would either make a holding attack on the Boer left flank while Colley stormed the Nek, or support him with a parallel advance in the direction of Wakker-stroom. Colley's letter next went on to impress Wood with the urgency of getting the reinforcements up to the front as soon as possible, explaining that, 'if all goes well here, and the troops are not unduly delayed by the rains, I hope to be in a position to move forward about the 20th [of February], about which time your troops will be beginning to assemble at New-castle. . . .'[1] 'You will also, I am sure,' the letter ended breath-lessly, 'understand that I mean to take the Nek myself!' Clearly Sir George had every intention of revenging his first defeat in person, and meant to keep Sir Evelyn in his place.

But the hard fact was that during the Majuba campaign, none of the plans formulated by General Colley ever signified very much, because sooner or later he was always obliged to respond instead to the enemy's movements. So now, at the beginning of the second week in February, all his strategic schemes were upset by an unexpected reverse.

It occurred on a stony plateau seven miles south of Mount Prospect. For some time the General, as we have seen, had been sensitive about the vulnerability of his communications; his uneasiness increased when an escort accompanying the mail from Mount Prospect to Newcastle on the 7th February was ambushed by an enemy patrol, which apparently had been dispatched from the main Boer Laager to harass the British rear. This was intolerable. As the General explained to Lady Colley, 'I was bound not to submit to be blockaded without an attempt to open the road.'[2] He decided to discourage further raids by leading a demonstration in force half-way down to Newcastle next day, and to take the opportunity of escorting a convoy of supplies back to Mount Prospect. Rather more than 300 men were detailed for the duty. One can only conclude that the General's reason for not entrusting the command of this small force to a subordinate officer was his desire to monopolise any chance of military distinction that might be going.

At 8 o'clock on the morning of the 8th, accordingly, five companies of the 60th Rifles, accompanied by thirty-eight mounted infantry and four horse-drawn guns marched out of Mount Prospect Camp and took the main road south. There is a depressing resemblance in this march commanded by General Colley to that earlier one which Colonel Anstruther had led to Bronkhorst Spruit. No one anticipated meeting any serious resistance. It was a glorious sunny morning; the men were in good spirits and calling out cheerfully to each other; they were travelling light, and carried neither food nor water, since the General expected to have the troops back in camp that same afternoon.

After a march of about five miles, the column came to a double drift just above the confluence of the Ingogo and Harte rivers. Here Colley prudently detached a company of the Rifles and two mountain guns to command the fords from a spur to the north. After a short rest, the remaining soldiers splashed through the two rivers and then trudged up the slope beyond towards a small plateau, named Schuin's Hoogte, less than two miles away. It was the place where the postal party had been intercepted the day before.

It was just midday when the leading files breasted the rise on to the plateau, and pulled up short as they caught sight of about a hundred enemy horsemen 1,000 yards away to the right. The Boers were reined-in on the open slope beyond a small ravine, and they were far too tempting a target for the English gunners to ignore. The expectant column waited as the two nine-pounders were wheeled round in the centre of the plateau, and hurriedly unlimbered. Everyone there knew exactly what would happen next; a few shells would pitch into the timorous Boers, who would then take alarm and disperse.

If the battery commander on Schuin's Hoogte had been more accurate in calculating his ranges, that is probably what would have occurred, and the story of the Majuba campaign might well have run on a different course; unfortunately the first shell screamed high above the horsemen and burst some distance away on the slope beyond. And the incredible followed: instead of hurriedly withdrawing, the Boers rode 'boldly' forward into the attack. After reaching the cover of the ravine, they dismounted and opened a heavy rifle fire on the startled soldiers, while pushing round their right flank to envelop the plateau.

Colley realised with a shock that he had lost the initiative. Before the trap closed, there was just time for him to send two horsemen racing back to Mount Prospect with orders for three companies of the 58th to reinforce the Rifles covering the double drift. A hasty examination of the plateau where he had halted then revealed it to be roughly four acres in extent and triangular in shape. The ground was fairly level, grown over with short grass, and fringed with granite boulders. The riflemen were feverishly extended round the perimeter of the plateau as the enemy fire swept through them. By 12.30 the engagement had become general.

At first the guns exposed in the centre of the position bore the brunt of the Boer rifle fire, and the gunners lost so heavily that volunteers from the infantry had to be called on to replace them. An attempt by Brownlow's handful of mounted infantry to roll up the enemy flank ended with the loss of nearly all their horses, the wounded animals, according to one eye-witness 'galloping madly about the battlefield in all directions, kicking and lashing out at everything in their way, and trampling on the dead and some of the unfortunate wounded' until a merciful shot brought them down.[1] After that both sides settled down to a vicious shooting match, where all the advantages lay with the Boers. They had good cover in long tombookie grass in which were scattered numerous boulders, whereas the redcoats were exposed and vulnerable against the skyline.

The two sides were fairly evenly matched in numbers. Smit, who commanded the Boers on Schuin's Hoogte, engaged nearly 200 men to begin with, and during the course of the afternoon received about 100 reinforcements from the Nek. But so rapid was their rate of fire that Colley was convinced he was facing odds of three to one.

The greatest danger for the British lay at the eastern apex of their position where, at about 3 p.m., the Boers advancing up a re-entrant were able to establish themselves on the lip of the plateau and search it with destructive fire. Colley met the threat by pushing seventy men of the Rifles towards the enemy across 600 yards of open ground. They were led by one of his staff, Captain MacGregor. In 1881 officers still went to war mounted on chargers, and predictably MacGregor was shot from his horse before he had gone very far, and most of his men fell with him. But a heroic handful, advancing farther than Colley had intended, gained the doubtful cover of a small outcrop of rock a mere sixty yards from the most advanced Boers, and there they stayed for the remainder of the day. Only sixteen men of the company survived the fight, but without question they saved it from becoming a massacre.

The hot afternoon wore on very slowly, and all the time Colley's situation grew more critical. The soldiers were plagued by thirst, their casualties mounted continuously, and the guns on which so much confidence had been placed were silenced, probably for the first time in history, by concentrated small-arms fire. A bayonet charge to drive off the Boers was discussed, but the General, mindful of the way the 58th had been slaughtered at Laing's Nek, shrank from another such sacrifice. By late afternoon it seemed that only annihilation or surrender awaited the parched soldiers on Schuin's Hoogte.

But at about five o'clock a gleam of hope flickered when the volume of enemy rifle-fire slackened and the Boers were seen to be collecting their wounded. Admittedly the onslaught was vigorously renewed a little later after Smit had received reinforcements, but towards sundown the enemy were seen by the incredulous troops to be disengaging. Thunder-clouds had been banking up for some time, and now heavy rain began to fall. It seemed a blessing to the thirsty wounded, but many of them who would otherwise have survived, died that night lying out in the cold and wet. As darkness came down the fight on Schuin's Hoogte sputtered out. By 7 p.m. only the weird moaning of dying men broke the sullen rain-filled silence which covered the battlefield.

General Colley was huddled, white-faced and anxious, in the

centre of the plateau, soaked through and chilled, and finding what shelter he could behind the carcass of a dead horse. Flashes of lightning and the occasional appearance of the moon from behind a cloud lit up the apprehensive faces around him. He rejected a suggestion to build an earthwork and fight it out with the Boers from behind its cover next morning. What weighed with him was the knowledge that his poorly-manned camp at Mount Prospect would fall an easy prey to a deter-mined enemy attack unless he got what remained of his troops back to it without delay. This would mean abandoning his wounded and attempting a desperate night march with highly-strung troops. The risks he knew would be tremendous, and as Colley himself confided to an enterprising (although now anxious) journalist who had accompanied the expedition, he expected some 'rough work'[1] on the way. An alert enemy would be able to cut his force to pieces during the withdrawal, and the Ingogo might well have risen too high to be forded. These were the chances he had to face. But Colley accepted them. The men were quietly withdrawn from the perimeter and mustered in a hollow square; the few remaining horses were harnessed to the guns. Then, soon after 9 p.m., the soldiers stumbled off in the direction of the double-drift, wisely giving a wide berth to the main road. The protesting cries of the wounded were slowly lost in the noise of the gathering storm, as the soldiers squelched in pitch darkness through the muddy veld. After about two hours they heard the sound of the river in spate ahead of them and, while they got what rest they could on the wet grass, a patrol was sent creeping down to recon-noitre the Ingogo. Another two hours went by before it returned with news that was both good and bad: the enemy unaccountably had neglected to defend the drift; but no contact had been made with the British troops on the spur beyond.

The Boers, as it turned out later, had missed the chance of a decisive victory. A party of Smit's horsemen sent out to seize the drift during the fight on the plateau had been driven off by the soldiers on the spur above, who had just been reinforced by the timely arrival of the 58th from Mount Prospect. Smit did not think it mattered very much. He believed that Colley had no horses left to drag his guns away, and was certain the Rifles had been too badly mauled to risk a retirement in the face of an intact enemy. And such was his confidence that after posting a few vedettes to watch the British position, Smit allowed his burghers to scatter and seek shelter from the storm. They were all confident they would find Colley's men in their old position on the plateau next morning, where they could be finished off at leisure. It was the only real mistake the Boer leaders made during the whole Majuba campaign.

As it was, only sheer unadulterated good luck saved the British from destruction. The noise of the storm protected them when they slipped away from Schuin's Hoogte in the darkness; and although the Ingogo River had risen as high as the soldiers' shoulders, by linking arms they were able to ford it with the loss of only eight men swept away by the flood. By midnight they were across the river and comparatively safe. In a stupor of fatigue the soldiers dragged themselves on up the five long miles to Mount Prospect, obliged to pull the guns themselves when the horses refused to move them any farther. It was a 'most horrid spell on foot,'[1] Carter the war correspondent remembered later, and 'the most dreadful spell of work I ever accomplished.'[2] Daylight was on them before the last straggler tottered into camp. But nearly half of the three hundred men who had marched out so cheerily from Mount Prospect twenty-two hours earlier had been lost; the Boers had suffered only eight men killed and ten wounded. It was with considerable understatement that Carter ended his dispatch with the admission that 'It is impossible to regard the affair other than as a reverse for our side.'[3]

Much to Colley's relief, the four companies posted above the double-drift had enjoyed a peaceful night, quite ignorant of their comrades' plight, or even that they had passed them in the darkness. Daybreak brought them sudden recognition of their dangerous exposure, but they were able to make a hurried withdrawal without molestation.

But for Colley it had been a very near thing. Only the Boers' overconfidence had saved his entire force from annihilation. Now it was so depleted he could do little but hold his camp. He could not spare men even to patrol his communications, and Wood's advancing reinforcements would have to look after themselves. The unhappy Colley was well aware he would have to accept censure for abandoning his wounded, and he was terribly disillusioned by the failure of his vaunted guns; they had even proved a liability: 'I don't think you will miss artillery much,' he informed Evelyn Wood, who was without artillery and expected to be made to fight his way up to Mount Prospect; for the Boers, Colley explained, 'keep too good cover or move too rapidly and in too loose order to give it much chance.'[1] It was an opinion which was to influence him later against carrying guns up Majuba when he seized that hill. And after Ingogo Colley knew deep personal sorrow since nearly all his remaining Staff Officers had been lost: 'It is altogether too sad', he lamented to his wife on the day following the battle, 'every personal friend I have made here gone.'[2]

Although Sir George had been shocked by the Boers' mobility, cool courage and instinctive aptitude for war, he could at least comfort himself by remembering his own soldiers' remarkable steadiness during that bitter afternoon on the plateau above the Ingogo. And it was a tribute to his singularly winning personality that even after this second disastrous engagement, morale at beleaguered Mount Prospect still remained high.

The last acts of the small drama on Schuin's Hoogte were as dismal as any that had gone before. On the day following the battle, burial and stretcher parties under a flag of truce, went down the road to the Ingogo again in pouring rain to inter all the dead and attend the wounded who had survived a hideous night. But social custom of that time demanded that officers should be buried separately from common soldiers, and several days later a second party marched back to the plateau, shooed away the vultures, brushed off the flies, disinterred the officers' bodies and brought them back to the trim little cemetery at Mount Prospect which now was filling up so rapidly.

Colley's New Plan

On the same afternoon that Colley's men were fighting for their lives on Schuin's Hoogte, Lord Kimberley sat at his desk in the Colonial Office composing a telegram. He had come from a Cabinet meeting where the latest messages from that most indefatigable of mediators, President Brand, had been discussed. In them the President had pointed out that one of the obstacles to peace was the Boer leaders' fear that they might afterwards be discriminated against as rebels, and he suggested that an assurance of pardons for them would advance the chances of reaching a settlement. In the Cabinet room it had been very obvious that Gladstone's Ministry was now only too anxious to find a way to end the war and restore independence to the Transvaal, provided this could be reconciled with British responsibility for a beneficent native policy, and accomplished without losing too much face. Before the ministers rose, the Colonial Secretary had been directed to reply to Brand, through Colley, in such conciliatory terms that the door would be opened a little farther for negotiations. Now Kimberley sat frowning over his desk as he searched his mind for the right words to use; at last he was satisfied. 'Inform President Brand,' his cable instructed Sir George Colley, 'that Her Majesty's Government will be ready to give all reasonable guarantees as to treatment of Boers after submission, if they ceased from armed opposition, and that a scheme will be framed for the permanent friendly settlement of difficulties'. [1]

Kimberley went home then, sure that after this exercise in statesmanship a compromise peace, based on the suggestions he had already confided to Sir Evelyn Wood, had been made possible. He awakened next morning to read about the beating the Natal Field Force had taken the day before above the Ingogo. It was all very embarrassing; he knew the Government would find it difficult to go on making conciliatory noises now their troops had suffered another ignominious defeat.

Colley's military reputation, already lowered by Laing's Nek, took a further downward plunge after Ingogo. The Natal

Press in particular was after his blood. The General attempted to justify his losses by suggesting he had so mauled the Boers that the British reinforcements recently arrived from India could now march safely up to Mount Prospect. But the excuse ceased to be plausible when Smit's commando appeared a few days later, practically unscathed, in the Biggarsberg mid-way between Ladysmith and Newcastle. Here in broken country ideally suited to defence, Smit was in a position to dispute the passage of Evelyn Wood's column. In the event he declined to attack the reinforcements, though not because the fight at Ingogo had weakened him, but because Wood's column was unexpectedly strong: two infantry battalions and a fresh cavalry regiment were too formidable a force for even his 200 burghers to tackle.

It was during these days of march and countermarch that Kruger surprised everyone by making his first peaceful gesture since the outbreak of hostilities. On 12th February he addressed a long letter to General Colley. After reciting a few passages from the the familiar litany of the Boers' grievances which had compelled them 'to proceed in a bloody combat',[1] he went on to say that his people were so certain the English Government would be on their side if it knew the true facts, that they would be prepared to submit the Transvaal's case to a Royal Commission of Inquiry, and abide by its findings. He made the single proviso, however, that 'Your Excellency commands that Her Majesty's troops be immediately withdrawn from our country'.[2] In other words, if the Imperial military garrisons in the Transvaal surrendered, he was prepared to accept a peace on terms formulated by the British.

The differences between London and Heidelberg were slowly being narrowed down, and now it needed only some small compromise by one side or the other for a peaceful settlement to be reached. But Colley, for one, was not prepared to make that compromise. He dutifully transmitted the purport of Kruger's suggestions to Whitehall but, remembering Kimberley's snub of the week before, did not answer them, and went on with his plans to renew the offensive.

On the 13th, the telegraph line from Mount Prospect to Newcastle was cut by the Boers. It was a particularly awkward time for this to happen; Colley now found himself out of touch with the three regiments marching up the road to his relief. On the following night the General attempted to re-establish contact with Newcastle by risking a ride across country under cover of darkness, but he was back in camp four hours later having encountered an enemy patrol. On the 16th, however, Colley got a letter through to Wood, and it is of some interest to us because it shows that, despite Kruger's overture, Sir George still had every intention of attacking the Boers again before the politicians made peace. After warning Wood in his letter that he would find the Boers 'not at all wanting in courage either in galloping boldly under fire to seize an advantageous position, or in creeping close up to our skirmishing line whenever the ground gives any chance; and very accurate shooters', he went on to say: 'I shall of course be glad to receive reinforcements which will enable us to do something more than just hold our camp.'[1]

Meanwhile the English Cabinet had met again to consider Kruger's offer. Although the demand for the withdrawal of the British garrisons from the Transvaal as a preliminary to negotiations was considered inadmissible, the Ministry replied to Heidelberg with a qualified acceptance of his suggestion that the case be submitted to a Royal Commission. 'Inform Kruger', Kimberley cabled Colley on the 16th February, 'that if the Boers will desist from armed opposition we shall be quite ready to appoint Commissioners with extensive powers' to develop a scheme for settlement,[2] and he went on to authorise Colley to agree to an immediate suspension of hostilities if these terms were acceptable to the Boers. This cable was accompanied by one from the War Office respecting 'the interval before reply from Boers is received', which concluded: 'We do not bind your discretion, but we are anxious for your making arrangements to avoid effusion of blood.'[3]

Concerned perhaps lest Colley would disregard its pacific intentions, the Cabinet's cable was copied to Sir Evelyn Wood and to President Brand. Wood's copy was waiting for him when he hurried ahead of his troops into Newcastle on 17th February. Colley was there, too, having safely sneaked through the Boer patrols the night before.

Only now, for the first time, did Colley learn from Sir Evelyn of Kimberley's scheme for settling the Transvaal problem by partition, and he was consumed with indignation. For it appeared that the Imperial Government had launched itself irrevocably on to the slippery slope of appeasement, and (without a word to him) had decided to divide the Transvaal into two, restoring independence to its 'purely Dutch districts', while retaining sovereignty over 'the native border districts'.[1] Such a recipe for peace, Colley insisted, was morally dishonourable but impractical too, and he proceeded to fire off protests to London, both by mail and cable.

'Either accept the Boer programme and give them back the Republic "under British protection"', he suggested 'very earnestly' to Kimberley on the 18th, 'or adhere to the annexation but give them a more liberal constitution'.[2] And he buttressed his advice with a threat of resignation which he knew could not fail to embarrass the Government. Nor was it an idle threat: 'I would rather resign', he told Lady Colley in a letter written on the same day, 'than carry out the scheme.'[3] He provides us with fresh evidence of his real intentions in the same letter to his wife, for it continues: 'I know that by the time this reaches home I shall have broken the back of the military resistance, and my words may carry more weight than they would just now.'[4] It seemed absurd to George Colley that after going to the trouble of assembling a force strong enough to reassert its authority over the Transvaal, Gladstone's Government were preparing to compromise with the rebels. He had every intention of defeating them first, and the means were rapidly becoming available. Newcastle was crowded now with fresh troops from India: a splendid regiment of Hussars had already ridden in, followed by the 2/60th Rifles, a sister regiment to the one which had fought at Ingogo; behind them came a Naval Brigade commanded by Colley's close friend,

Commander Romilly, and the 92nd Gordon Highlanders, fresh from a triumphal campaign in Afghanistan. In addition another 1,500 soldiers were either due to land at Durban, or were already on their way up country. Power to crush the Boer rebellion had returned to Sir George Colley again, and with that power had come his increased intransigence and determination to outwit the defeatist authorities at home. On the 19th, after sending Wood off on a long reconnaissance towards Wakkerstroom to ascertain whether the enemy defences on the Nek could be turned from that direction, Colley in his best ironic manner fired off another cable concerning the armistice terms to Lord Kimberley: 'Am I to leave Laing's Nek in Natal territory in Boer occupation', he inquired sarcastically, 'and our garrisons isolated and short of provisions, or occupy former and relieve latter?'[1]

The Colonial Secretary refused to rise to the bait; 'the garrisons', he cabled back soberly, 'should be free to provision themselves and peaceful intercourse with them allowed, but we do not mean that you should march to the relief of garrisons, or occupy Laing's Nek if arrangement proceeds.'[2] This was clear enough, but unfortunately Kimberley added a sentence to his message which gave General Colley an opportunity to sabotage the negotiations: referring to the previous proposals for an armistice, he told the General to 'fix reasonable time within which answer must be sent by Boers'.[3]

Monday, the 21st February, was a day of great activity for Sir George Colley in Newcastle. For three weeks he had moved about in a mood of black depression as the wounds inflicted by his military failures began to smart and stiffen; now he believed he could see a way to heal them.

He began the morning by protesting afresh to Lord Kimberley regarding his partition scheme, and something of his morbid concern about his own reputation comes out in this letter when he makes the penitential observation: 'I cannot but perceive that my failure at Laing's Nek has added considerably —I regret to say it—to your lordship's difficulties in effecting a settlement.'[4] But there was nowhere a suggestion that he was already thinking of redeeming that 'failure'. The General next clapped his helmet on his head and went outside to see Sir Evelyn Wood off to Pietermaritzburg. Possibly he felt a little embarrassed as he did so, but during the last few days he had found it awkward having to listen to his brother officer's continual harping about a soldier's duty to obey his Government's instructions however distasteful they might be, especially as Wood had generously agreed to serve under him in Natal—although his senior in the Army List, and possessed of an outstanding military reputation. Now Colley effectively freed himself from Sir Evelyn's unwelcome advice by dispatching him down country again with the flimsy excuse that he was to hasten the arrival of more reinforcements at Newcastle. As Carter, a correspondent with Colley's little army, pointed out, 'the idea that Sir Evelyn Wood's presence at Pietermaritzburg would accelerate by even five minutes the arrival at Newcastle of troops on the march between Durban and the Biggarsberg, is so supremely absurd that it is not worth a moment's consideration.' Indeed, after thinking it over for some time, Carter concluded that this awkwardly punctilious colleague had been got out of the way (on an errand which could have been performed by a junior staff officer) because 'Sir George Colley meant to take Laing's Nek single-handed,'[1] and had no intention of being deflected from his purpose or sharing its rewards.

Colley next clarified his thoughts that morning by informing Sir Garnet Wolseley of the local military situation, and by grumbling in another letter to his wife of his fears that 'the Government seem so anxious to come to terms that I expect to hear of their giving in to everything the Boers demand.'[2] It was time then for the General to inspect the newly-arrived troops, and his voice rang through the muddy streets of Newcastle in a harangue which warned them about the prowess of 'the enemy you are now going against'.[3] Then Colley shut himself up in his room again, and at last his busy pen turned to drafting out Lord Kimberley's armistice proposals of the 16th for transmission to the Boers. To these proposals he succeeded in giving a subtle hardening of tone which he knew would make them less acceptable. 'I am to inform you', he wrote, 'that on the Boers now in arms against Her Majesty's authority ceasing armed opposition, Her Majesty's Government will be ready to appoint a Commission, with large powers, who may develop the scheme referred to in Lord Kimberley's telegram of 8th inst.'[1] The sting came in the third paragraph: 'I am to add', Colley wrote, as though these were the exact words of the Cabinet's instruction to him, 'that upon this proposal being accepted within forty-eight hours, I have authority to agree to a suspension of hostilities on our part.'[2]

With that last sentence Colley had successfully twisted Kimberley's message into something very close to an ultimatum. In view of its consequences it is only fair to add that according to one authority—Norris–Newman—this sentence was a shade less peremptory, and read: 'I must add that if this proposal is accepted within forty-eight hours from and after the receipt of this letter, I have empowered a cessation of hostilities on our side.'[3] But whichever way it is looked at, the conclusion is inescapable that Colley deliberately stiffened his instructions to allow the Boers a 'reasonable time' to answer the proposals, into a demand for an answer 'within forty-eight hours', which as he very well knew was a physical impossibility.

The subsequent history of this letter, on which so much depended, was to be the subject of a good deal of controversy later on, and it is as well here to anticipate events by considering what happened to it. Colley wrote it, as we have seen, at Newcastle on the 21st February. For the next three days it remained in his pocket. It was still there on the 23rd when the General rode back to Mount Prospect, and was not delivered to Smit until the following morning. In acknowledging the *démarche*, Smit informed the British General in writing that Vice-President Kruger could not possibly receive it for some time as he had left the Nek for Heidelberg, 120 miles away: he went on to say it would accordingly be at least four days before an answer could be expected. On the 26th the Boer General learned that Kruger was even farther away than he had thought, having been summoned to deal with some crisis in the remote village of Rustenburg, and Smit hastened to inform Mount Prospect that with the best intentions in the world a still longer delay must be anticipated before Kruger's reply came in. Having given these explanations, the Boers appear to have assumed that the forty-eight hours allowed them for an answer would be indefinitely extended; certainly when the British General made an offensive move against them that same night, they felt he had acted in bad faith.

Altogether Monday, the 21st February, as we have seen, had been a crowded day for General Colley, and the letters he wrote at Newcastle in the course of it give us a very fair insight into the way his mind was working.

We know much less, however, about his thoughts during the next two days—the 22nd and 23rd of Febraury, 1881—but we can make a very shrewd guess at them by studying his movements. They at least are straightforward enough. In the early hours of the 22nd, Colley left Newcastle for Mount Prospect at the head of 1,800 men. A screen of Hussars and Mounted Police rode in front and on both flanks; they were followed by battalions of both the Gordon Highlanders and the 2/60th Rifles; then came the Naval Brigade and a long line of transport wagons stretching back over two miles of road.

There seems no reason to doubt that Colley that day intended to concentrate this powerful force at Mount Prospect, and use it to make another frontal assault on the enemy position at the Nek if the Boers rejected the 'ultimatum' he was carrying in his pocket. By the time he was ready to put in this attack he expected Wood would have brought enough troops up to Newcastle to support him with a demonstration which would draw off at least some of Joubert's men from his objective.

Colley's head must have been full of these strategic plans as his column tramped across the plain north of Newcastle, and went on up the slope to Schuin's Hoogte, and past the piles of stones which marked the graves of the soldiers who had fallen there two weeks before. Only a little farther on they came to the double drift and laagered by the river for the night.

It was here at the Ingogo on the evening of 22nd February

68

that General Colley heard—and perhaps saw—something which made him alter his tactical plans.

He heard that the enemy defence works round Laing's Nek had been very greatly strengthened during his few days' absence in Newcastle. Clearly a frontal attack now would prove extremely costly, and Colley reluctantly decided that the British main effort after all would have to be made from Newcastle towards Wakkerstroom—which of course meant relegating the troops based on Mount Prospect to a subordinate role.

Accordingly next morning the 2/60th followed by most of the Hussars were ordered to return to Newcastle, while the General continued the march northwards with the Highlanders whose diminished function now would be to guarantee the security of the standing camp at Mount Prospect.

As he rode up the road towards Laing's Nek, Colley, no doubt, was in a very disgruntled mood: his decision, however militarily correct it might be, nevertheless meant that the glory of beating the Boers out of their defence line would now go not to him but to Sir Evelyn Wood. But Colley's discontent must have lightened as the morning sun brought out all the colours of Majuba in front. His imagination, as happens to all travellers on this road, could not fail to have been caught and kindled by the texture and theatrical silhouette of this hill towering above every other eminence in the landscape. Inevitably as he rode on Majuba loomed ever larger on the skyline and ever larger in his thoughts. And the realisation could have come almost haphazardly to Colley that the seizure of this hill would be a far easier way of outflanking the enemy position than a complicated operation towards Wakkerstroom.

Historians will aver that the conception was triggered off by the General's recollection of Sir Frederick Robert's night march to seize a hill named Peiwar Kotal in Afghanistan two years before; it had turned the enemy line and at the time Colley had been full of admiration for the brilliance of this exploit. The romanticist, however, will insist that the thing was destined.

The thought of capturing Majuba was no more than a passing notion at first in Colley's mind, but it grew slowly into a resolve, and then was elaborated into a plan. But until he came close up under the hill it still remained a judicious plan. 'It was not', recorded Colonel Stewart who had just joined Sir George as his Chief of Staff, 'in the first instance the General's intention to have endeavoured to obtain possession of the hill until considerable reinforcements had reached him . . . from Newcastle.'[1] But as he came nearer to Laing's Nek, a fatal sense of urgency was grafted on to Colley's design. For he saw that the enemy entrenchments were beginning to extend on to the slopes of Majuba. Clearly if the hill was to be seized, it would have to be done quickly.

And if it were done very quickly, Colley was satisfied it could be done bloodlessly, and would not constitute a hostile act. Majuba, after all, was situated in Natal which was indisputably British territory, and it had never been permanently held by the Boers.

By the time Sir George rode into Mount Prospect Camp on the 23rd, he could think of little else but his flash of inspiration about Majuba Hill. After seeing the Highlanders settled in their new quarters, he sat down to report his arrival at the front to London. And he was not dissembling when he assured the War Office, 'I would not without strong reason undertake any operation likely to bring on another engagement,' or even when he went on to write, 'I may have to seize some ground which has hitherto been practically unoccupied by either party, lying between the Nek and our camp.'[2] For he was genuine in his belief that what he intended to do could not be construed as an aggressive action.

Next morning—the 24th February—Colley at last dispatched his forty-eight-hour 'ultimatum' to the Boers on the Nek. Then he rode round the extreme left flank of the enemy position, far into the Transvaal, with a small escort of Hussars. The reconnaissance was designed to allow him to study the farther face of Majuba, and he hoped it might also distract the Boers' attention from their right flank. What the General saw of the hill was reassuring. From his vantage point behind the enemy's line, its north-eastern face appeared to be scarcely less precipitous than the one opposite Mount Prospect, and he came to the conclusion that once three or four hundred soldiers were established on the summit of Majuba, they would not only be in an impregnable position, but would oblige the Boers to abandon Laing's Nek, or at least compel them to fight for it at a grave disadvantage.

As he rode back that afternoon to his camp, General Colley's mind was made up. He would seize the hill during the night of 26th/27th February when his forty-eight-hour time-limit had expired. The eviction of the enemy from Natal which was bound to follow would restore his military reputation before the meddlesome politicians of Whitehall were able to conclude a dishonourable peace.

It was the kind of plan which historians would describe as that of a military genius if it succeeded, and that of a reckless fool if it failed. But Colley never thought of it as being rash to the point of foolhardiness; he did not recognise even its most obvious flaws; he appreciated neither that he was attempting the *coup* with too few men, nor that he was mounting it prematurely. Worse still, he completely failed to make any arrangements to exploit the success if he succeeded in capturing the summit.

'The enterprise was that of a madman,'[1] the forthright David Cromb wrote a little later of the General's design: most military critics since then have agreed with him. And it is just possible that Colley was indeed deranged at the time. When Sir William Butler, the General's most eloquent apologist, wrote Colley's biography, he covertly questioned 'the balance of his mind'[2] during that last week in February. Sir Percival Marling towards the end of his life similarly remembered of Colley that 'after Ingogo he hardly ever slept at all, and used to be writing, always writing, in his tent half the night'. Again, Rider Haggard, who was ostrich-farming near Newcastle in 1881 and in close touch with the Imperial troops, believed Colley was 'not himself'[3] when he planned the operation; while another writer —Vulliamy—has suggested that the General's judgement was affected then 'by personal criticism and reproach of a peculiarly

intimate nature'.[1] The clear implication here is that Lady Colley
goaded her husband into attempting to retrieve his reputation
before hostilities ended. Conceivably she did: she had already
told him she was 'very angry and bitter at the peace party';[2]
and, after all, in rather similar circumstances Lord Chelmsford
had been incited to revenge Isandhlwana by a relative's
telegraph: 'For God's sake do something stop Wolseley
supersedes you stop.'

The evidence for such an accusation, however, would appear
so flimsy as to be almost ludicrous were it not corroborated to
some extent by contemporary local gossip. The tale is referred
to in the book based on the regimental records of the Gordon
Highlanders, which was written to disclaim that unit's responsibility for the Majuba disaster. The relevant passage reads: 'A
lady, very closely related to Sir George Colley, was at Newcastle, a town a few miles distant from the camp. After General
Colley's death it is stated, upon authority that need not be
questioned, that a letter from this lady was found on his body
to the effect that Colley now had his opportunity (General
Wood being absent), and that if he did not do something she
would "never speak to him again".'[3]

But this particular morsel of scandal is neither important nor
particularly relevant. For, in order to find the real motive which
drove him up Majuba, there is no need to look beyond Sir
George Colley's own haunting fear of being pilloried for the
rest of his life as a military failure. The fairest conclusion we can
reach is that Colley, ardent all his life for distinction, had in
1881 been tried beyond his strength in its vain pursuit. Ultimately frustration made him lose both his patience and his
judgement; and with them he lost his life.

The Miraculous Seizure of Majuba

Men at Mount Prospect afterwards remembered Friday the
25th of February as a particularly restful day. Only Colonel
Stewart had been told anything about the General's intentions
for the following night, and their secret had been well kept.
The two men worked out the details of the operation like

conspirators. Strategically, it was to be an attempt to turn the Boer line; tactically they proposed to make a daring flank march at night. One of their chief anxieties concerned the possibility of meeting resistance at the top of Majuba. Colley knew the Boers used the summit as an observation post, sending a piquet up the hill each morning and withdrawing it again at dusk; but he was not quite certain whether the enemy patrolled the hill during the night. To find out, a Zulu scout was sent off to climb Majuba on the Friday evening with orders to report back next morning.

Even on Saturday no one in the camp suspected anything unusual was being prepared. There was, instead, an air of gaiety about Mount Prospect. The regimental band of the 58th, and the Gordons' pipers happened to be in remarkably good form, and the men lounged about in the bright sunshine, joking together, singing their favourite tunes and playing cricket 'with pick handles for bats, and ammunition boxes for wickets'.[1]

The high-spirited Highlanders poked fun at the younger soldiers of the 58th and 60th, telling them how they would deal with the Boers when they got the chance. Scarcely anyone, except the war correspondent Thomas Carter, noticed that Colley and Stewart were spending the day engrossed in the scrutiny of Majuba Hill, three or four miles away. Stewart was propped up with pillows on his bed peering at it so intently through his binoculars that Carter thought its outline 'must have become indelibly stamped on his mind',[2] and when Carter questioned the Colonel about his interest, he did not find Stewart's answer particularly plausible, that 'he was trying to discover whether the Boers had any guns there'.

Majuba Hill, the focus of the two men's attention, is not just another of the table-topped kopjes which are such a common feature of the South African scene. It stands out boldly from the rolling companion hills which are thrust out from the Drakensberg mountains into the tilted plain of northern Natal like a rampart to guard the Transvaal. Moreover, Majuba wears a discordant aura of elemental power about itself, as though sensitive of its renown and conscious it has been set apart as a hill of destiny. And there is this that is unique about Majuba: its curious outline, once seen, can be summoned back into the mind again in the most precise detail and with the puniest effort of memory, whereas only the haziest recollection is retained of far more famous eminences. Nor can one ever become tired of looking at Majuba, not so much because of its beauty, but because of its changing character. For this hill possesses something of the infinite variety of the sea. That is why the traveller on the trunk road into the Transvaal, whose eye ranges over the pearly-grey wall of the accompanying Drakensberg Mountains and the billowing green confusion of kopjes at their feet, finds his attention almost unconsciously straying back again and again to this separate brooding hill to seek some new aspect of its strange quality.

Majuba is a mountain rather than a hill; its summit stands more than 6,000 feet above sea-level and 2,000 feet higher than the western end of Laing's Nek. But convention, perhaps in deference to the mightier pinnacles of the nearby Drakensberg, has labelled it a hill, and as Majuba Hill it will now forever be known to history.

In shape, Majuba resembles a monstrous decapitated pyramid. Rising from a broad base, its slopes are marked by parallel strata of sandstone and shale, which form alternate encircling terraces and short precipitous cliffs. The hill's faces are broken here and there by rocky buttresses and deep re-entrants. In wet weather a fine white mist crowns its summit; during this Saturday in the February of 1881 it was sufficiently dense at first to disconcert Colley and Stewart peering at it through their glasses. But presently a wind came up which set the clouds racing away and revealed to them all Majuba's step-like scarps and wooded ravines in remarkably clear detail. Every rock and every crevice stood out then in sharp relief through the wonderfully lucid air of southern Africa which follows rain. To the two officers at Mount Prospect it appeared the easiest thing in the world to climb and seize this hill which was the key to the whole Boer position. It seemed of little account to them, that although they had stared its slopes almost out of countenance, they had not the slightest knowledge of the curious configuration of its summit.

On this Saturday, Majuba was a word that had little meaning except to the few Boers who farmed the valleys at its foot, and the Kaffirs who had given the hill its name because of some fancied resemblance in its chequered sides to a native dovecot. But within twenty-four hours Majuba was to become a ghostly possession of both the British and the Afrikaner people, a name which would remind one of a national humiliation, and for the other conjure up splendid memories for pride to fatten on.

To the south the great hill looks over the lush green fertility of Natal; on the northern side it towers above the lion-coloured veld of the Transvaal. And there is this other oddity about Majuba Hill: to the casual observer, something akin to an optical illusion makes it appear equally steep all round, whereas, although the ascent from Mount Prospect is sharp and arduous, on the north the veld sweeps half way up its slope, and the climb from the Boer laagers was far less formidable than the one from the south. This, to his cost, Colley had failed to appreciate when he rode into the Transvaal three days earlier.

'One might have thought', Carter felt, as he became increasingly intrigued during the afternoon by the two officers' continued absorption in the hill, that 'they had never seen it before.'[1] Presently, as he watched, a kaffir approached them and pointed towards Majuba. Colley quickly knocked down his hand and looked around as though concerned lest anyone had appreciated the significance of the gesture. But the report the scout brought back was reassuring: he had seen no Boers on the summit that night, and water could be easily found there.

As the evening shadows lengthened across the slopes of Majuba, another member of the staff, Major Fraser, was called to join the two engrossed men, and was entrusted with the secret of the operation. Standing together there, they saw the tiny figures of the enemy patrol outlined on the skyline for a moment, and watched them begin to descend the hill. The three officers exchanged significant looks, then turned without a word to go inside the mess tent and join the rest of Colley's staff at dinner.

This, one of those present recalled afterwards, was a particularly cheerful meal; there was no trace of strain, or hint that anything out of the ordinary was going to happen. Only when dinner was over a little before 8 p.m. did a shower of orders suddenly descend upon the startled staff. They were to be carried out by mouth-to-mouth commands. Three companies of the Gordons, two of the 3/60th Rifles, two of the 58th* and a section of the Naval Brigade under Commander Romilly, were to parade in an hour and a half's time in full marching order. Each man was to carry three days' rations, full water-bottles, seventy rounds of Martini-Henri ammunition, rolled greatcoat and water-proof sheet. The regimental officers concerned were to ensure that each company was in possession of a full complement of entrenching tools; finally, the men were to be warned that no lights were to be struck and the utmost quiet was to be observed.

Having watched his officers scatter through the camp in a whispered babble of conjecture, Colley went alone into his tent and settled down to write a letter to his wife. Its tone suggests he had already faintly heard the beat of shadowy wings above him: 'I am going out tonight to try and seize the Majuba Hill, which commands the right of the Boer position,' he told Lady Colley, 'and leave this behind in case I should not return to tell you how very dearly I love you and what a happiness you have been to me.'[1] Next, his strange presentiment of death set him explaining the rules he had tried to observe through life, his feelings about the future, and his present sense of frustration. 'How I wish I could believe the stories of meeting again hereafter,' he wrote then, 'but it is no good complaining because things are not as one might wish—one must only brace oneself to meet them as they are.' He concluded: 'think lovingly and sadly, but not too sadly or hopelessly of your affectionate husband . . . G. P. C.'

* According to Carter (p. 254) there were three companies of the 58th and one Rifle Company in the task force, but here he seems to have been mistaken.

76

As he put down his pen, the buglers outside sounded 'lights out' through Mount Prospect, and the notes carried clear across to the enemy lines. The Boer sentries, as they went their rounds, saw darkness envelop the British camp. Far below them, his letter sealed, Colley walked towards the parade ground where his men were forming up. 'Those who were going', noted one journalist, 'were in high glee—those who were to remain behind were bemoaning their "hard lines".' The General stopped for a brief aside to the camp chaplain, asking him to ensure that Bruce Hamilton, his brother-in-law, who was serving him as A.D.C., should not be roused until he had gone. 'There seems a kind of fatality about my staff,' he explained; 'if anything were to happen to him, it would kill his sister'.[1]

Then the line of soldiers snapped to attention as the General came up to them through the darkness, and amid a flurry of salutes, he formally handed over command of the camp to Colonel Bond, the next senior officer, with hardly a word of explanation about what he was going to do.

There was a vague suggestion about this, Colley's last parade, that its 600 participants were going off on some swashbuckling enterprise. They were 'a scratch lot of soldiers and sailors', as Lieutenant Ian Hamilton recalled afterwards; for the troops were drawn from four separate units. All of them were weighed down with equipment, and all were in reckless high spirits at the prospect of a fight. There were 170 redcoats of the 58th, and similar numbers of the Rifles and Gordon Highlanders. At the rear stood Commander Romilly with 64 blue-jacketed sailors from the *Boadicea*. In the darkness, and from all sides of the drill ground, their comrades crowded up to stare enviously and in silence at the task force.

From the facile vantage point of hindsight, we can appreciate now that Colley would have been far wiser to have taken a single battalion rather than this composite force to seize Majuba: it lacked homogeneity and *esprit de corps*; there was no hierarchy of officers down which command would automatically pass in the event of casualties; nor was there a single regimental commander known to all the troops, round whom they could rally in a crisis. Indeed, it is quite possible that the story of the coming operation would have had a different ending if the Gordons alone, under their own Colonel, had been engaged on it; they were fresh, tough and battle-confident.

There has been a good deal of speculation about Colley's reasons for embarking on the enterprise with such a 'scratch lot' of soldiers. The most likely explanation is that he had not forgotten his promise to allow the 58th to revenge their previous defeat, and it would have been invidious to take them while leaving out the Rifles and at least a party of sailors. Certainly this was the opinion of the correspondent from the *Standard* who put it this way: 'General Colley, feeling himself assured of success, wished that every regiment in his camp might have a share in the victory he expected to win. He hoped that the 58th would wipe out Laing's Nek, and the Rifles the Ingogo.'[1] But it is just possible there was instead a political angle to the General's selection of the force. For years now, Sir Garnet Wolseley and Sir Frederick Roberts had been engaged in a bitter dispute over the organisation of the British army: Wolseley was anxious that it be recruited on a short-term basis; while Roberts favoured the old system whereby the ranks were filled with long-service soldiers, in which opinion he was strongly supported by the Duke of Cambridge, who had a great distaste for Wolseley's 'damned new-fangled notions'.[2] Any success by a long-service unit like the Gordons, after short-service troops had failed so miserably in two previous engagements, would have mortified the 'Wolseley ring'; such an embarrassment could only be avoided if Colley selected a mixed force for the final crucial operation.

Different authorities have given discrepant figures for the number of soldiers who marched out of Mount Prospect with Colley that Saturday night. The confusion no doubt arose from the fact that during the march which followed, detachments were dropped off by the General to keep open his lines of communication, and also because an additional company of the Rifles left the camp later on during the night to join one of these detachments. Carter, who accompanied the march, tells us that Colley's original column numbered 554 fighting men and nearly 50 'medical staff and kaffir bearers';[1] of these, he says, about 200 soldiers were left in two makeshift laagers below the hill. His figure approximates that given by Ian Hamilton, who says 365 men were on the summit when the fighting began. A recent writer, however, states this latter number should be 414.[2] Norris-Newman, on the other hand, puts the original British strength at 728 officers and men, and this figure is the one officially accepted.[3]

Another controversial point about Colley's force concerns the question of whether or not it was accompanied by artillery. Norris-Newman and Aylward—both of whom were special correspondents with the Boers—maintain that the column started off with two mountain guns, which had to be left behind at the bottom of the hill.[4] No other witness, however, supports their statements; and anyone who knows its slopes can hardly believe that Colley thought he could get even mountain guns up to the summit of Majuba at night with the resources at his disposal. But the difficulty of the terrain in no way exonerates him for neglecting to take any rocket-tubes with him on the expedition: determined men could have man-handled them up the hill in the darkness, and they would have played a decisive part in the operation. Even a Gatling gun on the summit might have prevented the coming disaster; but Cameron, another journalist who accompanied the column, is alone in stating that the Naval Brigade pulled one along with them at the beginning of the march, but were obliged to abandon it before they had got very far.[5]

It was nearly 10 o'clock when Colley mounted his horse and, accompanied by his staff and two Zulu guides, rode out of the camp at the head of his task force. The 58th had the place of honour in the van; then came the Rifles and the Highlanders, while the sailors brought up the rear. It was an eerie march; an uneasy tension gripped the men as they peered about them through the darkness. 'The night was bright', Major Fraser tells us, 'but there was no moon.'[6] The soldiers could make out the massive bulks of Imquela Mountain and Majuba against the stars as they trudged down to the main road, crossed it, and continued up a native track on the far side. The General had considered directing his approach to Majuba along the road itself; it was the easiest way, but as it would have taken him close to O'Neill's farm, which was frequently patrolled by the enemy, he had wisely chosen a more circuitous route. Fraser and the two guides now took the lead and, having gained a ledge on the slope of Imquela, wheeled right along it towards Majuba. Presently a halt was called and the two companies of the Rifles were detached with casual orders to cover the general movement and to send a patrol to the top of Imquela in the morning.

The soldiers now found themselves trudging along a kaffir path, so narrow that they were obliged to move in single file. 'On one side', a survivor recorded, 'was a deep precipice, on the other an impassable wall of rock,'[1] time was lost when the slope levelled out and sections of the column kept straying. Colley's time-table began to slip behind schedule, but although the march was more anxious now, it was still not pressed. At midnight Fraser ordered another halt on a spur close to the base of Majuba. A full hour went by before all the stragglers had been brought in; it was not a comfortable respite for the soldiers; a keen north wind was blowing from the plain, and the sound of barking dogs at O'Neill's farm below, suggesting that the alarm had been given, set everyone's nerves on edge. Before the column moved on again a company of the Highlanders under Captain Robertson was detached on the spur with vague instructions to 'dig as good a trench as time would permit of',[2] and the officers' chargers were left in his care. The remaining soldiers then began the ascent proper of Majuba. The path mounted very steeply up the south-west flank of the hill, and progress became extremely slow. Yet the tired men's spirits rose; at least they knew where they were going now, and the whispered word 'Majuba!' ran right down the snake-like column.

Ian Hamilton remembered the next few hours as 'a terrible

climb', so steep that the men had to stop every few steps to regain their breath. 'It is a perfect mystery to me', another officer of the Gordons wrote later, 'how men with pouches full of ammunition, carrying rolled blankets and great-coat, and three days' rations could have got up . . . on a pitch dark night.'[1] In some places they were obliged to crawl on hands and knees, hauling themselves up by tussocks of grass. In the darkness they stumbled over brushwood and rocks; every now and then someone would fall down with an unnerving clatter of equipment; cries of 'put out that light' when a groping hand lit a match, would bring the column to a cringing halt as the soldiers froze in their tracks expecting to be shattered by an enemy volley. Hamilton tells us that fantastic fears would ripple down the line when a tree or boulder was mistaken for a waiting enemy sniper, and once 'there was a sort of splintering up of the head of the column and a horrid stifled sort of muttering, "here they come—fix bayonets".'[2]

Colley feared that because of these 'almost impossible slopes' his soldiers would be caught by daybreak exposed and helpless on the hillside. He became terribly anxious when the guides halted to argue between themselves and then confessed they had lost their way. It was the darkest hour of the night. The dawn was very near. But after casting about again, and toiling up another steep spur, Fraser scrambled at last on to the summit of Majuba. A hasty reconnaissance showed him it was unoccupied. It was not quite four in the morning, but another hour and more slipped by, and the leaden sky was already streaked with dawn before the last panting Highlander reached the top and threw himself flat on the grass.

Colley himself was still comparatively fresh when he followed Fraser on to the plateau of Majuba: he had ridden for a good deal of the way, and at the base of the hill had taken the precaution of changing his heavy boots for slippers which, according to Vulliamy, looked like 'white tennis shoes'.[3] And he had good cause to congratulate himself. Astonishingly, even incredibly, he had got a column of 365 soldiers to the summit of the main bastion of the Boer defences without losing a single man. It was a remarkable achievement. Ian Hamilton was not alone in thinking that this was 'surely a shining feat of arms and extraordinarily reminiscent of Wolfe's climb by night up on to the heights of Abraham.'[1]

A journalist, watching the General, afterwards remembered his 'anxious and care-worn countenance' (in which he nevertheless detected 'traces of deep, although suppressed, excitement'),[2] as Sir George quietly directed the groups of men arriving on the summit to deploy along its brim. They spread out more or less evenly round it at about twelve-pace intervals; no attempt was made by the officers to concentrate them at the more obviously vulnerable parts of the perimeter, or to extend them across the comparatively inaccessible sectors. The most cautious of the soldiers began to build protective stone schanzes; but the majority strolled over to the northern face of the hill and gloated over the twinkling lights of the enemy laagers behind Laing's Nek 2,000 feet below. Had they been within earshot they would have heard the murmur of reverent prayers and hymns of praise greeting the dawn in the enemy camp. For this was Sunday morning, the 27th February, 1881.

It was an exciting moment. Carter later remembered exulting that 'there was our enemy *at our mercy,* and unaware of our proximity to them'.[3] The British soldiers found they were perched on top of what seemed an impregnable natural citadel dominating the Boer defences. 'We could stay here for ever,'[4] Colley remarked to Stewart after posting the soldiers to his satisfaction; and a correspondent was certain 'nothing in the world but hunger could turn them off the position they had occupied'.[5] Indeed, so confident was the General in the position's natural strength, that he issued no orders for the soldiers to dig themselves in. 'The men were too exhausted to intrench', explained Fraser later in his official report, 'and hardly fit to fight.'[6]

Among the mistakes General Colley made during the Majuba campaign—and there were many of them—this failure to set his men digging trenches was the least excusable of them all. It was gross and it was fatal. Apologists have tried to excuse

the lapse by insisting with Fraser that the men were so worn
out by their arduous climb that they had to be rested first.
Carter thus tells us that 'the poor fellows, heavily laden with
their accoutrements, provisions, ammunition, and arms, were
well-nigh exhausted'.[1] But Colley's fatherly regard for his
men that morning should have been more concerned with their
safety than with their comfort; without doubt they would have
found the necessary reserves of strength to dig trenches if he
had called on them for another effort, and it is by no means
certain they had even approached the limit of their endurance.
Hamilton, for instance, makes a point of saying that his
Gordons were 'too excited to feel fatigue and I saw no signs of
it'.[2] He assures us, too, that 'I have never felt less tired in my
life than when I looked at the Boer army lying at our feet; and
my men felt the same'.[3] Indeed, he accounted Colley's failure
to order entrenchments to be dug 'a crime, not so much against
the science of war as against the art of war'.[4] This opinion was
supported by Colonel Stewart who three months later wrote:
'I need scarcely say that I utterly disagree with the view of the
men being exhausted,' and added, 'the march was not rapid nor
over severe. Sir George was not a bit tired.'[5]

Colley's second grievous error that morning was a failure to
explain the situation to his soldiers, or speak to them of the
opportunities that lay before them. Hamilton has something to
say about this, too: 'No one had been told what was happening,'
he protests; 'no one ever said those few burning words due to
the men from their Commander even if only to let them understand how much they had accomplished and how vital it was
that they should see it through.'[6] In fact the soldiers on the
hill remained ignorant of the General's intentions during the
remainder of that fatal day.

To signal his arrival on Majuba's summit to Mount Prospect,
Colley ordered a flare to be lit on that part of the hillside hidden
from the enemy. Then, as the sky over the hills on the other
side of the Buffalo River began to pale, he turned for the first
time to study the configuration of the hilltop he had seized. It
was a spacious saucer-like plateau, about 10 acres in extent,

and triangular in shape with its apex pointing north-west and the base facing a little east of south towards Mount Prospect. A well-defined rim, marked by rocky outcrops and about three quarters of a mile in circumference, ran right round the summit. From this outer edge the ground descended gently inwards to form a grassy basin, in places 40 feet deep and strewn with boulders. The depressed plateau was roughly bisected by a low ridge running more or less parallel to the north-eastern face of the triangle; it joined two kopjes which stood opposite each other on the rim and were known to the natives as 'Majuba's breasts'. That morning the soldiers named these hillocks after the officers who commanded the contingents posted on them. The western 'breast'—Macdonald's Kopje— —was a prominent conical feature and represented the true summit of the hill. That on the right—Hay's Kopje—was broken with boulders, and rose only a little higher than the rim. The lowest and most protected part of the basin lay immediately to the south of the low ridge that traversed it: this hollow was about 200 yards long and 60 yards wide: in it Colley established his headquarters; in it too the doctors busied themselves setting up a first-aid station, and two shallow wells were dug 'so we had something' Carter gaily noted 'to dilute our gin'.

Investigating further in the grey light, Colley and Stewart found that the two faces of the hill adjoining its south-west shoulder, up which the difficult ascent had been made, 'seemed altogether impracticable'[1] to attacking troops. What was less obvious about these precipitous slopes was that they were so broken by terraces and ravines, and so overgrown with shrubs and trees, that their lower approaches were concealed from the view of men standing on the summit.

The rim of these two sides coincided with the summit of the steep ascent of the hill; but the north-eastern face, which over-looked Laing's Nek, was somewhat different. From the rim here, the ground did not at once descend sharply but sloped down quite gently to a well-marked outer brow before plung-ing abruptly to a wide flat terrace some two-thirds of the way up Majuba, and which from above appeared to end in a second precipitous drop. It was clear that here the rim did not command the ascent as on the other two sides of the hill, and the Highlanders posted to this sector were ordered to leave its natural cover for the exposed grassy slope immediately above the outer brow.

In the growing light two isolated spurs were now seen to project bastion-like from the hill's summit. One near the south-west angle, where the men had ascended, was detached from the main mass of the hill and stood set apart from it like a miniature Gibraltar. The second outlying spur was situated beyond the northern angle; it was a bare round knoll tufted with short grass and standing only a little lower than the rim, to which it was joined by a saddle less than seventy yards across. It was beyond the tactical capacity of the General and his staff officers to recognise that this knoll was the key to Majuba; but they did appreciate that it commanded the last hundred feet of the hill's north-eastern face, and they pushed out a handful of the Gordons to occupy it. Thereafter it was known to the soldiers as 'Gordons' Knoll'.

It was full daylight now, and the men were beginning to enjoy themselves. A mocking group of Highlanders perched themselves on the skyline overlooking the Boer camp, waving their fists and shouting taunts of 'Come up here, you beggar.'[1] One man even loosed off a round at an unsuspecting enemy patrol riding round the hill, although it was well out of rifle range. Nothing more provocative could have been imagined, and it is curious that General Colley allowed it to occur after taking such immense pains to conduct the night march secretly. But such was everyone's confidence now in the impregnability of Majuba and discipline had become so lax, that an enemy attack was positively invited. 'Had orders been issued for every man to lie close', reported one of the war correspondents, who had looked forward to seeing the Boer's customary morning patrol walk into a trap, 'we might have captured the first arrivals without a shot being fired.'[2]

For some time Colley's staff officers on Majuba busied themselves sorting out the men into their proper units. The northern half of the hilltop was allotted to the Gordons, the 58th were posted along its southern face, while the Naval Brigade held the area round the southern angle.

After some prompting by the subalterns of the 92nd and 58th, a few more perfunctory schanzes were erected, but the sailors on their own initiative set up formidable stone defences overlooking the ascent route; these sangars were never tested in the action that followed, and still stand on Majuba today looking as though they had only just been built. Then, satisfied that the whole perimeter was covered (although without particular regard to the vulnerability of its various sections), a large reserve was told off to rest in the sheltered hollow beside the wells.

The soldiers were excited and full of expectation. Carter says everyone was sure the mere occupation of Majuba Hill was but part of a larger scheme, and that soon they would watch 'the artillery advance within range of the Nek, supported by the remainder of the 58th, the Highlanders, and the 3/60th. We should see the guns begin to pound away . . . the Hussars and Infantry would advance to the assault, and at the same moment part of our forces would descend from the position we held, and our movement spread dismay and terror amongst the enemy, and there would then be a general stampede of the Boers. . . . The Boers were going to do nothing but run all day. . . .'[1]

And the opening was there: unfortunately no other tactical stroke had been set in motion to exploit it. Worse still, a strange and fatal listlessness had overwhelmed their General. He was not even concerned with improving his position. When Stewart spoke to him about building some defences on the plateau, he lackadaisically dismissed the idea with the reply that the troops were still tired and needed further rest. A similar suggestion from an A.D.C. prompted Sir George to reply they 'did not require anything very substantial, as it was only against rifle fire'.[2] No attempt was made to occupy the slopes of the hill below the rim, nor even to investigate their character. Indeed, judging from the sketch-map drawn later by Fraser to illustrate

GORDON'S KNOLL WITH RIDGE IMMEDIATELY BELOW

MACDONALD'S KOPJE

PRECIPICES ON LINE OF HIGHLANDERS' RETREAT

BRITISH ASCENT ROUTE

Majuba Hill from the west

Gordons' Knoll from Macdonald's Kopje

Aerial view of Majuba Hill

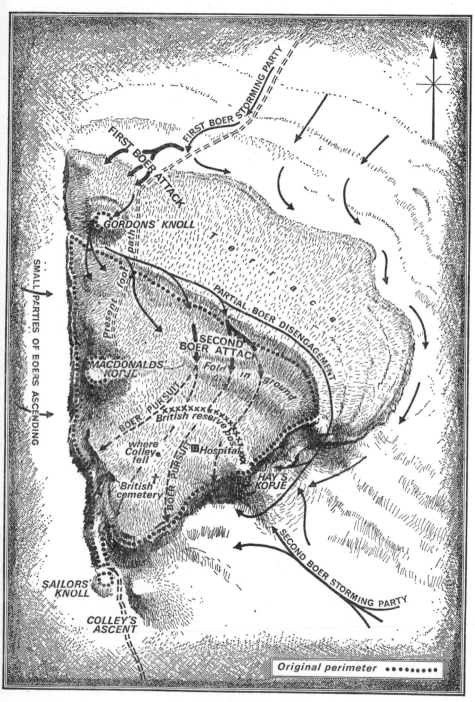

Summit of Majuba Hill

his official report, the staff officers gained only the haziest idea of the configuration of the hill's summit, and none at all of its approaches.* No one dreamt, as the soldiers basked in the sunshine, and the golden hours of safety slipped away, that the enemy had already begun their counter-attack, and were even then circuiting and climbing the hill unseen by its defenders. Least suspicious of all was General Colley as he perambulated round the perimeter, telling the soldiers nothing of his intentions, and replying to their questions with only, 'all I ask you is to hold this hill three days'.[1] He was satisfied that the first part of his gamble had paid off. But it was only the first part. Before he had been on top of Majuba for one hour, Colley had already lost the initiative; and to make matters worse, he had not the slightest idea he had lost it.

The Ignominious Rout

Below on Laing's Nek the Boers had been alerted to their danger. According to Afrikaner tradition, news of the British capture of the hill was carried to them by a Mrs. de Jager, who lived on a farm under its western slopes; it further maintains that (despite the darkness) she saw a Union Jack unfurled on its summit. But the likelihood is that her attention was attracted by the flare lit on Colley's orders to announce the occupation of his objective to Mount Prospect. At all events, Mrs. de Jager saddled her pony and galloped through the night down the Oliviers Hoek road to the Boer camps. Commandant-General Joubert, who tells us that at this time he had been 'lulled . . . to an unwise unsuspiciousness',[2] had yet passed a sleepless night pondering over his reply to Brand's latest peace proposals. He goes on to say he was in his tent 'still

* The erroneous orientation of Fraser's map was probably due to his compass having been affected by the abundant iron-stone in Majuba Hill. Both Colley's two staff officers survived the rout, and lay low on the hillside until darkness. Stewart's compass was so badly affected that he blundered into the enemy lines and was captured. Fraser, however, seems to have learned to discount the discrepancies of his compass, and, using glow worms to illuminate its face, found his way back to Mount Prospect. To facilitate physical descriptions of Majuba Hill in this book, the author has slightly altered the meridian on accompanying maps so as to suggest that one face of the hill ran directly north and south.

sitting writing, and the sun had just risen, when it was reported to me that the troops were coming up the right-hand hill.'[1]

At first the Boer Commandant-General took the moving figures, who were in fact the last stragglers of Colley's column, to be mountain goats. He was only set right when Mrs. Joubert, who like many of the burghers' wives had accompanied her husband to the war, sarcastically enquired, 'since when have mountain goats been dressed in red tunics?' There was no need for him to pass the warning on to his men: the injudicious shot fired a little later, and the jeering Highlanders on the skyline, were all that was required to arouse them to the situation.

Joubert's first reaction was 'that everything was lost to us.'[2] And this was the feeling of most of his burghers, who hastily inspanned their wagons and vaulted on to their horses, abandoning the Nek defences in panicky expectation of a barrage of shells falling on them. Hamilton up on the hill 'could see the Boers streaming right out of their trenches back to their laagers',[3] and we know that they went with loud intimations to each other that the *Rooineks* deserved punishment not only for treacherously advancing during an armistice, but still more so for desecrating the Sabbath Day.

But when it dawned on them that they were not being fired at from cannons on Majuba after all, some of the retreating Boers reined in, and considered whether it might not be possible to retake the hill. It seemed a forlorn hope, but after riding into the main camp, they found that there plans were already being discussed for storming Majuba. Legend debates whether it was Joubert or his wife who had galvanised the burghers in the laager with a shouted, 'there are Englishmen now on the mountain; you must bring them down.'[4] But it was certainly the Commandant-General who used short impassioned words when he addressed a hastily convened council-of-war, and called for volunteers to dislodge the soldiers. An order sent horsemen galloping down the Newcastle road, and westward round the hill, to intercept any troops marching out of Mount Prospect, and to cut off the retreat of those already established on Majuba. Then General Smit was directed to storm the hill. Eighty young

men—perhaps a dozen more—who had volunteered for the
task were divided into three commandos under the leadership
of Commandants Stephanus Roos, D. Malan and Joachim
Ferreira. No time was lost. They whipped their horses as far as
they would go up the flanks of the hill; there they dismounted
and worked their way towards the summit to await further
orders. The other available burghers—for the most part older
men who were the more reliable shots—stationed themselves
round the base of Majuba and covered the assault with a
barrage of rifle-fire in much the same way as, during the Great
War, Generals used artillery concentrations to support their
infantry attacks.

What military genius possessed these burghers! What instinctive aptitude they had for war! Here were a few hundred
men prepared to assault a position which any professional
soldier of the time would have insisted was impregnable. Yet
everything was planned by Smit that morning with Napoleonic
facility and speed; it was then carried out with an exact precision scarcely equalled in the annals of warfare. As early as
6 a.m., a desultory fire had been opened from the foothills on
to the crown of Majuba, but it was heavy enough to make the
soldiers keep their heads down. Within an hour that fire had
become general and heavy. And all the time the storming parties
were methodically moving upwards, brilliantly handled, and
using cover with the utmost skill.

There was nothing hurried now about their attack; five full
hours went by before they had reached positions within striking
distance of the plateau. And all that time more burghers were
committed to the fight as it became clear that Mount Prospect
was giving no support to the British task force. Encouraged
by the example and apparent invulnerability of the first assault
commandos, they swarmed up after them until at a little before
one in the afternoon no less than 450 Boers stood poised and
ready to attack the summit.

'Beyond all our expectations', Joubert reported that evening,
in prose that reminds us of Cromwell's war dispatches, 'the
Lord assisted us, and we all ascribe it to the most wonderful

deliverances and help by an all-governing and mighty God. Our men climbed the mountain with a courage and energy beyond description.'[1]

While one commando scaled the hill on its western flank, and a second climbed up from the eastern side under Hay's Kopje, the main assault led by Roos approached Majuba from the north using the cover of a wooded ravine which points like a dagger at Gordons' Knoll. Half way up the hill this kloof peters out under a miniature cliff, and there the burghers rested, drank water from a spring and extended into skirmishing order. Clambering upwards again they came to a flat grassy terrace, in parts 400 yards wide; beyond it lay another steep ascent reaching to that part of the rim of the plateau held by the Highlanders. While a few burghers extended to the left and joined hands with those approaching Hay's Kopje, the majority inclined to the north where the terrace narrowed and led to a rocky fold in the hillside immediately below Gordons' Knoll. It was then about 11 o'clock in the morning.

In twos and threes, covered by intense rifle-fire, the burghers dashed across the narrow segment of the terrace and mustered under cover of this ridge on the drop of the hill. By early afternoon about sixty Boers were concentrated here waiting for the signal to begin the assault proper.

*

For nearly all the soldiers on the summit of Majuba, that Sunday morning had passed peacefully enough. Those on the perimeter amused themselves by taking pot shots at the few figures they saw flitting about on the slopes below, and complacently reported they were causing the enemy heavy casualties. The reserves in the hollow enjoyed a leisurely breakfast, after which most of them dropped off to sleep. The General occupied himself in sending off triumphant flag- and helio signals from the south-west angle of the plateau. At 8 a.m. Mount Prospect was instructed to inform Whitehall: 'Occupied Majuba Mountain last night. Immediately overlooking Boer position. Boers firing at us from below.'[2] Three-quarters of an

hour later the enemy's apparent evacuation of the Nek made
the General decide to advance his time-table. 'Order up 60th
and 15th Hussars from Newcastle,' he instructed Bond at
Mount Prospect, 'and try and get in tomorrow morning.'[1] At
9 a.m. there came a solicitous inquiry as to whether the
groceries and reserve ammunition ordered to be brought up by
mule had reached Captain Robertson's outpost at the bottom of
the hill; and half an hour later, having presumably received a
negative reply, there was an even more fatuous message: 'Send
out some rations to post with a troop of 15th Hussars. All very
comfortable. Boers wasting ammunition. One man wounded
in foot.'[1]

Some of the soldiers present, however, were less happy about
the way the situation was developing; they even confessed to
having misgivings about the General's lack of activity. It was
difficult for them to understand why there had been no
'follow up' to the seizure of the hill, and why it had not been
co-ordinated with an assault on the Nek. It seemed futile to
expect to achieve a decisive victory by sitting idly on a mountain top, yet that was precisely what their General seemed to be
doing. 'Why didn't we bring up the rocket-tubes or the
Gatlings?'[3] someone asked, and was only partly satisfied by an
assurance that probably they were already on their way.

What exactly were Colley's plans that day? It is difficult to be
quite certain because he divulged very little of them before he
died. The most anyone learned from him directly was: 'I mean
to take the hill, and hold it until the reinforcements come up.'[4]
He clearly anticipated it might be three days before these
reinforcements were brought up from Newcastle to clinch his
victory; he could hardly afford to wait longer, for that would
risk the unwelcome reappearance of Evelyn Wood at Mount
Prospect, possibly armed with instructions from London to
forbid any more forward moves.

But we do know that Colley intended to return to Mount
Prospect as soon as he was satisfied his task force was securely
established on Majuba, and that he proposed to leave Romilly
in temporary command of the summit. He foresaw no difficulty

about reaching the base camp, having manned two laagers to guard his communications. It is reasonable to assume he then intended to spend the following day, Monday, hauling mountain guns up the hill, while reinforcements marched to-wards the front from Newcastle and the rear echelons. By Tuesday, he anticipated, the presence of artillery above their position would enforce the Boer evacuation of Laing's Nek. If the threat of shell-fire failed to accomplish this, he then presumably intended to lead an infantry assault in person on the Nek, supporting it with a flank attack from Majuba, and following up the operation with a decisive cavalry pursuit. Either way it seemed to him he could not fail to dislodge the Boers and rehabilitate his reputation at the same time.

Early that Sunday morning, however, the General seems to have been surprised that the mere appearance on the hill of his soldiers, without any artillery support, had been sufficient to make the Boers start abandoning their defences; he had not anticipated this, but to take advantage of their withdrawal he decided to accelerate his programme, and ordered up the Hussars and 60th Rifles from Newcastle at once. It never entered his head that after their first alarm, the Boers would have the temerity to attack him on Majuba; when they did so, thanks to his muddled thinking, he fought the battle that ensued *en l'air,* with the large majority of his available troops either sitting uncommitted in the camp at Mount Prospect, or preparing for the march from Newcastle to his support. Major Hay, the officer commanding the Gordon Highlanders in the Majuba task force, puts his finger on Sir George's strategical mistake with his comment, 'the fact was, either he was a day late in sending for the Hussars and 60th, or he moved . . . a day too soon.'[1]

But General Colley's unfortunate reticence made him neglect to put even his second-in-command completely 'in the picture' by discussing his plans with him. That reticence stemmed from a twisted anxiety to appropriate every particle of credit from an operation whose success he believed at first to be assured. The corollary inevitably followed, and when the operation began to show signs of going wrong, the wretched man exhibited an almost pathological tendency to swing from sublime confidence to a profound pessimism, which made him quite incapable of rectifying his mistakes.

But this still lay ahead when, at about 11 a.m., the General stirred himself sufficiently to reconsider the question of building some strong points on the plateau. He strolled across to the corner of the hill overlooking the path up which the ascent had been made, and joined Commander Romilly there. After telling him he intended to return to the camp soon and would leave him in command on the summit, he fell to considering with him the best sites for three prospective small redoubts which would serve as rallying points in the event of an enemy night attack on Majuba.

After some discussion it was decided to build one on Macdonald's Kopje, another on the eastern corner of the hill above Laing's Nek, while the third would be set up where they were standing overlooking Mount Prospect. If these defences had been built, there is little doubt the coming tragedy would have been averted, even though they were too widely separated to give each other proper support. Careful study of the ground, however, might have shown the General and Romilly that a more rational plan would have been to throw up earth-works round a natural platform, some three hundred yards long and a hundred yards wide, which projects on to the south-western corner of the plateau from the southern brim. Had Colley's soldiers been concentrated there, leaving only a thin screen of riflemen on the perimeter to delay an enemy ascent, nothing would have ever turned them off Majuba.

But speculation on these lines is purely academic, for in the event no redoubts at all were built that morning by the British; the malignant fate which Colley had come to believe hung over his friends, struck at one of them even as his conversation with Romilly was in progress. A Boer marksman sneaking through the undergrowth of the ravine immediately below the place where the little group of officers were gesticulating on the skyline, fired at them from a range of over 900 yards. The odds against his hitting any of them were high, but his bullet mortally wounded Commander Romilly. It is interesting to speculate how the fortunes of the day might have been altered if anybody else but him had been shot. For Romilly was a man of sterling character, and not afraid to give General Colley advice. Everyone on the summit of Majuba was distressed to see him hit, especially as Sub-Lieutenant Scott and others who stood only four yards away reported having heard the bullet explode after passing into his stomach.[1] This later led to the angry accusation that the Boers used explosive bullets during the action, but there is little to support the charge. The 'explosion' Scott heard was probably caused by an ordinary bullet striking Romilly's spine.

Yet there still seemed no grounds for anxiety. Romilly's wounding was considered an unfortunate accident, and Colley apparently clung to his earlier belief that the enemy fire was intended to cover the withdrawal of their main body from the Nek. Although that fire had been maintained for five hours now, only four British soldiers had been hit, and there seemed no reason to doubt that the return fire had been more effective. Soon after 11 o'clock, a signal to Mount Prospect informed its commander and Whitehall that 'Boers still firing heavily on hill, but have broken up laager and begin to move away. I regret to say Commander Romilly dangerously wounded; other casualties, three men slightly wounded.'[2]

But the loss of his second-in-command, when its significance sank in, came as a shattering blow to Colley. Observers noticed that from now on he wore a 'grave and reserved expression'.[3] Worse, it deflected him from his purpose of rectifying the faulty disposition of his troops and setting up redoubts for their protection, since the site of one he had chosen was plainly exposed to enemy sniping. And Romilly's loss tumbled the General from confidence into his alternative mood of passive pessimism and foreboding. Few people on the top of Majuba at the time, however, realised this; all they knew was that the General had become even more reticent and evasive about the situation, as though he was still 'keeping something up his sleeve'. And although the slow doom that had been gathering over his task force all morning would overwhelm it within an hour, still no one even conceived of its approach.

Only just before noon was the first note of alarm sounded from the northern section of the British perimeter. The High-landers there were suddenly subjected to an extremely heavy and accurate rifle-fire, and it pinned them down so effectively that successive small parties of Boers were able to rush across the terrace below them without loss and gain the cover of the ridge immediately beneath Gordons' Knoll. Ian Hamilton, the subaltern in charge of this sector, was so concerned by the development that he ran through the enemy fire to acquaint the General with the gathering threat. He came upon Colley in the hollow behind the transverse ridge where the reserves numbering about 120 men were assembled, and he could not help noting they were 'very comfortably eating, sleeping or smoking'.[1]

Carter, who was sitting there with the reserves, gives us some idea of the soporific atmosphere that attended them at this time: he says that when another officer climbed down into the hollow to obtain a few men for some task, he 'had to make a good deal of noise to wake them up'.[2] The languor around him may have affected General Colley; at any rate he was unimpressed by Hamilton's report; he merely acknowledged it, and when a second uneasy Highland officer, Lieutenant Wright, ran up to the General with another warning, he was dismissed with only the usual civil intimation that he must 'hold the place three days'.[3]

Hamilton was not a man to be put off easily; during the next half hour he persisted in returning to Headquarters to report that the enemy were assembling in increasing numbers below, and out of sight of, his position. He spoke at first of 200 burghers being on the hill, and he returned some time later to say the number had grown to 350. But the staff did not seem particularly concerned. He was back once more, just before a quarter to one, to say he now estimated the number of enemy infiltrating towards the perimeter at 400. Hamilton tells us that on this occasion he went up to where Colley had been resting, and found 'he was asleep'; he goes on to say somewhat bleakly, 'and so I reported to Lt. Colonel—then Major—Hay commanding the regiment.'

It was now probably 12.45 p.m. (It may have been a little earlier, but from midday on it is difficult to frame an exact time-table for the action, since the men involved in it were very soon to be fighting for their lives, and all sense of time dissolved in the confusion.) The Boers by then had completed their dispositions; several hundred fighting men were poised to break into the English position, and their spearhead of about sixty burghers—those chosen for their knowledge of the terrain—were gathered immediately beneath Gordons' Knoll. For some time these men had been cautiously studying the movements of the kilted soldiers above them, who stood up every now and then to fire at the enemy riflemen they could see at the bottom of the hill. These Highlanders had no cover at all on that rounded promontory; nothing more exposed than their situation could be imagined, and they were fatally ignorant of the Boers' approach to within point-blank range of them. This was the critical moment of Smit's plan. At a signal the waiting burghers below the knoll stood up, stepped back, and 'all of a sudden'[1] fired a volley at the figures above. Most of the soldiers on Gordons' Knoll were killed at once; only two or three survivors ran back across the saddle in panic to the main position.

'It was such a fire as had not been heard as yet',[2] recalled Carter of that crucial fusillade. A few moments later the Boers had swarmed up from the ledge and established themselves on the knoll, whence they commanded the northern part of the British perimeter from a distance of only seventy yards. Tactical intuition had brought them to the weakest part of the British line, and by concentrating there, they now vastly outnumbered this sector's defenders. It was an opportunity of which they took swift advantage.

Colley, we read, was 'startled up from his sleep'[3] by the heavy burst of rifle-fire, but it seems to have been Stewart who was the first to appreciate the gravity of the situation; with

97

another officer he came running into the hollow, shouting for the reserves to follow him to the support of the threatened sector. But the men faltered. According to one onlooker, 'the soldiers moved forward but slowly and hesitatingly. It was only too evident they did not like the work before them.'[1] Carter tells us, too, that 'my impression at the time while looking on was, that there was a want of alacrity shown by the men which was not altogether reassuring. There was a good deal of shouting and ordering, "Now will you step up quick there!" by the officers, which was not unnecessary to the occasion.'[2] According to one scandalised reporter, there was even some 'pushing', before the soldiers could be persuaded to advance to the Highlanders' support, and when they went forward they seemed to be 'firing at random'. The same dilatoriness of the troops is described by Hamilton. 'I next saw our Reserve coming up,' he writes, 'blue-jackets, 58th and about ten men of ours. They had fixed cutlasses and bayonets, and I fancied by their manner that they must have been startled by being so suddenly hurried up—anyway I did not much like the way they came up.'[3]

The panic of the few survivors from the knoll by now had spread to the Highlanders whom they joined on the hill's northern brow. And when the enemy 'poured in a tremendous fire'[4] on them from their newly-won position, it stretched the power of their endurance far beyond anything the soldiers could stand. The Gordons during the next few minutes lost more than forty men: it was a tribute to the accuracy of the fire that assailed them that an officer who examined their bodies later recorded 'all were shot above the chest; in some men's heads I counted five or six bullet wounds.'[5] As one of the surviving officers tells us 'a general funk had become established';[6] at all events the surviving Highlanders wavered and fell back —and ran straight into the reserve troops as they came up the exposed inner slope of the basin. For a moment there was a feverish confusion: then, despite the officers' exhortations, every soldier on the northern section of the line bolted for the rear scarp of the plateau. Behind them, encouraged by Roos' shouts that the *Rooineks* were running, came the enemy, rifles at their shoulders, firing incessantly at the rout. The line of panic-stricken soldiers swept right past General Colley in the hollow, and he stared at them in bewilderment. The situation was beyond his understanding and, as it turned out, beyond his remedy.

The confusion as the frightened men stampeded past this central hollow is nicely conveyed in Carter's narrative: 'officers from every side who witnessed the affair', he writes, 'shouted frantically, "Rally on the right! Rally on the right!" That call was in everyone's mouth. The men in flight had their backs turned on the enemy; the "right" of those retreating was therefore really the left of our fighting line, which was the principal line of the enemy's attack.'[1]

The mass of soldiers who 'responded to the call', instead of reinforcing the vital British right flank where it rested on Hay's Kopje, thus found themselves crowding behind the western section of the ridge traversing the plateau; and there they huddled like a flock of frightened sheep.

It was now a little after one o'clock, and the first part of the Boer plan had been successfully executed: they had broken into the British position. It was difficult for Colley's men to understand exactly what was going on, but plainly their situation had suddenly changed from comparative security to one of extreme peril. Drifting rifle-smoke covered the summit of the hill, and eddied in the depressions like a heavy fog. Anyone who showed himself above the low ridge became a target for a dozen rifles. The scent of death and the acrid smell of smoke smarted in the soldiers' nostrils and mingled with the bitterness of fear in their mouths, for these men were very frightened now, and the will to fight was seeping out of them. A lull in the firing as the Boers consolidated their new position on the rim only seemed to heighten the tension. The British officers spent it fussing round the men who were crouching behind the ridge, trying to sort them out into their units and extend them towards both flanks. And quite calmly General Colley made use of the respite to size up the situation.

Without doubt it was an alarming one, but it was by no means hopeless. Nearly two hundred soldiers had rallied behind the ridge, and they were not in a bad defensive position. The ridge provided fair cover, especially as an outcrop of rocks and loose stones was scattered along its crest. On the left, the line reached nearly to Macdonald's Kopje, where twenty Highlanders were firmly established. This was a vital strongpoint since it commanded the frontal approach to Colley's new defence line. On the right flank the ridge rose up to Hay's Kopje overhanging the eastern face of the hill; this bastion, although equally important to the defence, was unfortunately less strongly held, and it was exposed to rifle-fire, not only from the burghers on the northern rim, but from those climbing up the eastern shoulder of the hill. Indeed the men on Hay's Kopje were already showing signs of irre-solution: stragglers kept coming down into the hollow with feeble excuses, and stayed to argue with the officers who tried to turn them back. And enemy pressure on this kopje was plainly mounting; if it were lost, the entire British line would be enfiladed and rendered untenable.

But Colley's more immediate danger seemed to lie in front. The curious configuration of this part of the summit subtly weakened his position; and the weakness was to prove dis-astrous. For the ground fell very gently inwards from the northern rim of the plateau to a small longitudinal depression just deep enough for a man stooping there to be concealed from the soldiers occupying the ridge; then it rose again to a fold in the ground almost imperceptible, but with an incline still steep enough to provide cover for prone men to approach to within forty yards of the new British position. Here was an opportunity that the Boers were quick to recognise and exploit; under a heavy covering fire they wriggled forward by sections through the slate-blue smoke, and soon sixty or seventy burghers were separated from Colley's men by only forty yards of flat glacis utterly devoid of cover.

The enfilading fire from Macdonald's Kopje which everyone had been confident would check any such forward movement from the rim by the Boers, was effectively neutralised by extremely accurate sniping from the western base of Majuba. It was an impressive demonstration of tactical co-operation between two widely separated bodies of Boers. As Roos reported later, they were able to 'shoot each other free.'[1] So heavy was the fire directed on the kopje that one observer afterwards noted that the rocks there were 'white with bullet marks.'[2] Lieutenant Macdonald, excusing his men's failure in preventing the Boer infiltration towards the ridge, afterwards merely commented, 'they could see us from all sides',[3] but Hamilton gives a rather fuller explanation for their ineffectiveness: 'Unfortunately the top of the koppie', he informs us, 'was quite narrow, so that as the men crawled up to the top to fire they were shot in the back by the Boers down in the plain or half way up the hill.'[4]

Once the Boers were situated at point blank range in front of the ridge, their barrage of rifle-fire grew heavier, its rate, accuracy and terrible clamour exaggerating the burghers' numbers to the soldiers. Enemy bullets passing above the British position were now falling among the 58th on the southern perimeter of the plateau, and some of these young soldiers, already unnerved by the fugitives who had rushed past them down the hill a few minutes earlier, left their posts and followed them back to Mount Prospect.

Colley's men behind the ridge were gripped by bleak pessimism. They had little to aim at; all they could see through the bank of dark smoke were the muzzles of a dozen or more enemy rifles projecting over the ground-fold in front of them. But a few of the officers thought they knew a way out of their critical situation—a bayonet charge. Hamilton was one of those who tried to organise a counter-attack, shouting for his platoon to fix bayonets, but he 'was stopped', he tells us, 'by Colonel Hay, my commanding officer, who thought there were too few men.' A bizarre episode then followed, for the unabashed young man 'ran down to General Colley, and saluting said, "I do hope, General, that you will let us have a charge, and that you will not think it presumption on my part to have come up and asked you." Sir George replied—"No presumption, Mr. Hamilton, but we will wait until the Boers advance on us, then give them a volley and charge".'[1]

A good deal of discussion afterwards centred round Sir George's refusal to allow this attempt to dislodge the enemy with the bayonet. After all, the soldiers outnumbered the enemy immediately opposed to them by nearly three to one, and practically the only tactical advantage they enjoyed over the burghers was their training in close-order fighting. The Boers dreaded the thought of a bayonet attack; it ran counter to what they considered was ethical in war, and it was their good fortune throughout this struggle for independence that— save for the abortive charge at Laing's Nek—they never had to face one. Unquestionably the English soldiers would have lost heavily in covering the forty yards that separated the two firing lines; but they would have been upon the burghers before they had had time to reload, and empty rifles make poor weapons against naked bayonets. Colley's apologists have suggested that the soldiers by this time were too demoralised to make a counter-attack; but this may be doubted. One war correspondent was 'sure the men would have responded'[2] to their officers' call for a charge, while Carter, when he watched the soldiers fixing bayonets, 'felt convinced that in two minutes that murderous fire would be silenced, and our men driving the foe helter-skelter down hill.'[3]

But it is only fair to add that, in Hay's more professional opinion, 'a charge under such circumstances would . . . have been madness, and could have done no good.'[4] And he seems to have had his General's ear at this stage of the battle. At all events if there was an opportunity it was lost when Colley forbade the attack. It was his last decision, and it may well have been as disastrous as any that had gone before.

Meanwhile the threat to the British right flank was developing with terrifying rapidity. The burghers who some time before had disengaged themselves from the frontal attack, by now had joined their comrades climbing up the wooded eastern slopes of the hill. They brought a heavy fire to bear on Hay's

A Boer artist's conception of the battle

Outside O'Neill's cottage, March 1881

Front row, left to right: Franz Joubert, General Piet Joubert, Pres. M. W. Pretorius, Vice-Pres. S. J. P. Kruger, Pres. J. Brand, Sir Evelyn Wood, V.C. (holding helmet), Capt. Roberts, Major Clark, 2nd Lieut. Hector Macdonald,

Kopje, and soon drove off most of its defenders. Desperate attempts were made to regain this vital feature, but the soldiers were reluctant to obey their officers' commands and leave the comparative shelter of the ridge. 'Discipline', explains Carter, 'was on the wane',[1] and Lord Napier later sadly summed up the situation by confessing that 'the stubbornness of the British soldier, which used to cover all the blunders of the Commanders can no longer be counted on.'[2]

'The scene was one of wild excitement' on the right flank now, according to Carter. '"Will you deploy there? Deploy!" was the call,' he tells us, 'of the leaders. . . . Colonel Stewart and Major Fraser, seeing the hesitation,' he goes on, 'stepped boldly, sword in one hand and revolver in the other, on the way and facing the men, called, "will you come on here. Will you come on?" Who it was in particular held back I defy anyone to say. I saw blue-jackets, redcoats, and brown coats (Highlanders) moving in ones and twos on their faces to where they were called from; but an insufficient number were willing to obey the command. There was a hanging back, a reluctance of others, which neither entreaties nor threats could move.'[3]

The soldiers' morale had run out. They were ready to quit. Suddenly, Carter tells us, a 'piercing cry of terror . . . rose from the line or group of infantry'[4] below the kopje. The soldiers threw down their weapons and stampeded for the rear, stupid with terror, and paying no heed to the officers who cursed and threatened them with their revolvers. Within minutes those who survived the following fire were streaming down the hillside. One cannot altogether blame them for their failure to fight it out: the disastrous course of events was utterly inexplicable to them; they had lost all confidence in their leaders; and finally, as one young burgher wrote later to his father, they had been swept by 'such terrific firing . . . that it is impossible to describe'.[5] As the men raced for the path they had used to ascend the hill, the Boers came swarming over the eastern rim of the plateau, picking them off 'like pigeons'[6] when the fugitives for a moment stood outlined on the skyline. The panic was infectious; the soldiers on the British left flank now began to waver. Carter heard shouts from it of 'what the devil are you doing? Come back, come back! I'll shoot you if you don't return.'[1] The attempts to steady them had not the slightest effect; the men on the left of the line joined the route 'with another despairing cry'. The whole summit now was crowded with fleeing men.

It was not yet fifteen minutes past one o'clock; hardly more than half an hour had passed since the battle proper had been joined with that annihilating fusillade on Gordons' Knoll. And it was all over now except for the killing. There was no attempt to rally. Only Macdonald's platoon perched on their steep kopje stood firm, but by now, of his original twenty men, eight were dead and only two unwounded, and they were quite powerless to check the pursuit. Colley was still alive, moving about alone behind the ridge as though in a trance. Close by stood Captain Maude, one of his staff officers, and two gallant surgeons who had remained at the Aid Post with the wounded.

How easy it is on the summit of Majuba, even after all these years, to visualise again the last moments of this battle. Through the swirling smoke a line of burghers comes skirmishing over the ridge, shooting continuously at the fugitives in their headlong flight. Everywhere men are running, and stumbling, and zigzagging, and throwing up their arms as bullets strike them. Panic-stricken soldiers hurl themselves over the hill's southern brink, with open mouths and wild cries scarcely heard above the din. 'Some rolled down the hill,' one eyewitness recalled, 'some slid down, whilst others hung on to grass and bushes.'[2] Many of them crashed down the precipices to their deaths, others writhed on the slopes with broken limbs; for days the bodies of Highlanders festooned the hill like a grisly necklace where they had been caught by the trees which had somehow taken root on its rocky soil. The victorious Boers came crowding after them to the edge of the plateau, shooting down the fugitives, as one of them remembered, 'like buck' which, he added, he found 'al te lekker'—'very nice'.

Many of the soldiers surrendered rather than run the gauntlet of the hail of bullets crashing down the hillside. Others hid in the undergrowth until the shooting stopped, and darkness allowed them to regain their lines. No one thought of firing back.

And how easy even now it is to conjure up the vision of General Colley, left behind by the mêlée, standing beside the ridge with 'a calm and collected demeanour'.[1] Deserted by all but Captain Maude, he turns heavily at last to follow the rout with slow disdainful steps as the Boers close in on him. Maude remained with him nearly to the end; he fell only a few moments before Colley himself died with a bullet through his head, not two hundred yards from the ridge where his men had made their last stand.

This is the accepted tableau of his end, and there is a good deal of evidence to support its veracity, even if it was perhaps 'touched up' a little in a pious desire to make the General's death not only heroic but pathetic.

But the nagging doubt remains that it was not quite the way the final drama of Majuba went.

For instance, some eyewitnesses insisted that when General Colley saw his right flank give way, he authorised the withdrawal of his remaining troops to a last-hope position on the southern rim of the plateau. Admittedly most of this evidence came from officers of the Gordon Highlanders who had every reason to represent their men as retiring in pursuance of orders to renew the engagement from a second line, rather than as fleeing in a desperate *sauve qui peut*. One of them, Hamilton, said he remembered Colley 'holding his revolver high over his head' shouting, 'either "Retire and hold by the ridge" or "Steady and hold by the ridge".'[2] Wright similarly reported hearing the General shouting: 'retire in as orderly a manner as you can' before the soldiers 'jumped up and ran to the rear', although he adds that 'General Colley never went himself when he said retire'.[3] Major Hays agrees that the General gave 'the order to retire',[4] while one of Colley's staff officers appeared to confirm this too when he wrote, 'General Colley seeing the small number of men remaining, and that these few were being mown down . . . gave the order for them to retire as best they could'.[1] Finally Carter, one of our most reliable witnesses of the battle, supported their statements when he telegraphed immediately after returning to Mount Prospect an account of the British General 'giving orders to cease firing'.[2]

This all seems reasonably conclusive, but in fact a larger weight of evidence suggests that when the British line gave way, Colley was too dazed by the rapidity and finality of the disaster to be capable of influencing its course, or even to save himself, and was killed before his perception sharpened.

'The General had turned last of all to walk after his retreating troops,' one journalist reported, 'when he was shot dead through the head.'[3] Mrs. Montague, who accompanied Lady Colley a few days later to her husband's grave, put it more bluntly when she affirmed, 'there seems no doubt he was left alone entirely,' and added bitterly, 'he could not run like all his men did. This comes of commanding boys instead of men'.[4] A correspondent with the Boers had this to say about Sir George's last moments: 'General Colley, after the troops broke, himself began to fly. He was about eight paces in the rear when he was shot. He was the last officer who turned'.[5] A wounded British corporal who lay nearby in the Aid Post gave a slightly different account of his death: 'the General', according to him, 'never moved from where he was when our men retired. He stood there trying to rally the men, and one of the Boers shot him straight in the forehead some time after the day was lost. Had he chosen to turn, he would have had as good a chance as anyone else of getting away.'[6] Colonel Stewart reported afterwards that he saw Colley with his sword in his hand 'walking slowly some twenty yards in front of the Boer line which was advancing and firing rapidly. I moved towards him for some two or three steps when I saw him fall.'[7] Finally, Commandant Roos told Evelyn Wood some days after the battle that he saw the General 'standing up facing the Boers just before he was shot.' From all these somewhat divergent accounts one obtains the picture of a man so distracted by events as to have become detached from them, and only solicitous for death.

This may not be the whole of the story, however, for other evidence exists to suggest that Colley was still alert enough to make an effort to surrender immediately before he was killed. Carter, for instance, after questioning survivors from both sides, became convinced the General held up a white handkerchief as a token of submission just before he was shot. Melton Prior, the well-known contributor to *The Illustrated London News* came to the same conclusion; while another eyewitness recorded that 'Colley was fine until the very last, when it became obvious that fighting was senseless and when he was asked to surrender. Whilst tying a handkerchief to his sword, a bullet hit him in the back of his head and killed him outright.'[1] Finally Lieutenant Wright concludes his statement already quoted with, 'when last seen alive, the General's head was uncovered, and he was waving a white handkerchief.'[2]

No less discrepant than the reports of Colley's last moments were the accounts of the manner of his death. But they are more easily explained. A bullet's entry wound is always smaller than the one made by its exit. As most laymen would have done, Carter jumped to the erroneous conclusion that the larger wound was the mortal one, and after examining the General's corpse he widely announced that 'the fatal wound was at the back of the head'.[3] Several other observers fell into the same error. But it is clear from Dr. Mahon's report that the General was not shot from behind: 'he was only wounded once,' he says, 'and through the top of the skull. Death must have been instantaneous. From the direction of the wound he must have been facing the Boers when hit.'[4] Commandant-General Joubert later said, 'the bullet which killed him struck the top of his forehead, and came out at the back of his head.'[5] And Lieutenant Wright corroborates this with his statement that 'the bullet went in at his right side, just over the eye, and made an enormous hole at the back of his head.'[6]

The Boers were tremendously impressed when they heard they had killed an English General. After the shooting had ceased, both Carter and Hamilton were taken in turn to identify the dead man. Carter lifted up the helmet which had been placed over Sir George's face and 'saw the features as calm and peaceful as if in the repose of sleep instead of death.'[1] Hamilton 'found him on his back in the very place [he] had last seen him. They had covered up his face with greatcoats taken from our dead.' He could not bring himself to uncover the dead man's features, but recognised him 'by his clothes and figure'. The scene haunted Hamilton for the rest of his long life; years afterwards he spoke movingly of 'Sir George Colley, stretched out, exactly as the effigy of a Knight lies in a cathedral, upon the flattened summit of Majuba. His face I have to imagine, for a cloak has been thrown over it, but that is one reason why I remember it the better, and the wound, though I saw it not. Had death so composed his limbs, or the pious hands of the foe? I know not. There he lay upon a site which might have been selected by Valkyries for a hero's grave, midway between the Transvaal and Natal with an eagle's outlook over both.'[2]

Today a small whitewashed cairn on the summit of Majuba marks the spot where Colley fell only a few yards from the ridge behind which his men rallied for their last stand. His body lies peacefully in the little cemetery at Mount Prospect, beside the bodies of his friends whom he had mourned during the campaign.

*

Later that Sunday afternoon when the summit of Majuba had been cleared and the last shot fired after the fleeing soldiers, Smit called his jubilant burghers to order. Some were dispatched to 'winkle out' the fugitives still hiding on the hillside, while others herded the prisoners already taken to the Boers' headquarters behind the Nek. Volunteers were then organised into a commando under Franz Joubert (of Bronkhorst Spruit fame), with orders to capture the two British laagers below the hill on the ridge leading to Imquela, and then to storm the standing camp at Mount Prospect. By late afternoon the plateau had been abandoned to the looters, the dead and the dying. The Boers had won an incredible victory at hardly any loss. They had killed or wounded or captured 280 British soldiers that day. The Gordons had suffered the most severely; of the 120

Highlanders who had climbed Majuba the night before, only twenty-four came off the hill unscathed. In contrast the Boers had lost only one man killed in the action, and five wounded, of whom one died later. Two of their horses had also been shot. It was a poor reflection on British marksmanship considering the thousands of rounds of ammunition which had been fired at them.

Those who have studied the approaches to Majuba will understand why the simple burghers who had stormed the hill ascribed their victory to a Higher Power. For it was a miracle of a kind. It was no wonder that Joubert in his official report suggested to the Triumvirate that 'this day may be considered for the future a day of thanksgiving and prayer'.[1] But perhaps it was Ferreira, who had led one of the assault groups up the hill, who best expressed his comrades' feelings about their victory over the British. 'I do acknowledge', he wrote, 'that it was not US who defeated them, but The Lord our God. It was completely impossible for humans alone and then to think we lost only one man. So no honour for humans. All honour to our Great General.'[2]

*

The military events which immediately followed the action on the summit of Majuba were something of an anticlimax. To complete their victory, the Boers still had to finish off the two detachments General Colley had left on the ridge below the hill, and storm the Mount Prospect camp. It was decided to deal with the laagers on the ridge first. It will be remembered that during Colley's night march, two companies of the 3/60th had been detached at the southern end of the ridge, and a single company of Highlanders commanded by Captain Robertson left on a spur immediately below Majuba. Smit was a man who believed in crowding a beaten enemy, and very soon Franz Joubert was leading his men down the hill to assault them, while a fresh commando, eager to share in the success (and in the loot), galloped hard from the Nek to attack Robertson's left flank.

But there was just a chance Robertson might be able to beat

them off. He had been reinforced during the night by a further company of the Rifles sent out from Mount Prospect, and about 11 a.m. on the 27th had wisely detained a troop of Hussars which had clattered into his entrenchment with rations intended for the troops on the summit. By the time the fight on Majuba had been fought and lost, he had over 150 men well dug in along the spur, while only a little more than a mile away a similar number of the Rifles were entrenched in a position to support him; moreover the artillery that even then was being advanced from Mount Prospect would provide him with a certain amount of covering fire. There was an opportunity here, and if it could be grasped, Robertson would be able to pluck at least a limited success from the catastrophic course of the battle. Admittedly the odds against him were high but the history of the British army was full of precedents of the kind: less than two years before, the successful defence of Rorke's Drift, for instance, had taken much of the bitterness out of a worse disaster at Isandhlwana. And a check to the Boers immediately after their success on Majuba would have long-range consequences.

Robertson accordingly sent a horseman tearing across to the Rifles' laager asking for reinforcements, and then turned to fight it out with the advancing commandos. His men were in good heart. 'I never saw men steadier,' one eyewitness recorded 'or more prepared to fight';[1] and Robertson to his dying day affirmed that, had he been properly supported, he would have turned a rout into a splendid victory.

But things did not happen that way. The bleakness of spirit which so often overwhelms the observers of disaster, had by now afflicted Colonel Bond, commanding at Mount Prospect: as the Boers closed in on Robertson's laager, a peremptory signal ordered him 'to retreat his force without delay'.[2] It is not easy to blame Bond for making this decision; perhaps it was the right one; as he saw it his duty was to concentrate all available troops in his now vulnerable camp, instead of exposing them piecemeal to defeat. But no excuse can be made for the pusillanimous commander of the Rifles entrenched farther down the ridge. He folded up. No attempt was made to assist Robertson, or support his withdrawal. His two companies simply vanished from their laager and reappeared intact a little later at Mount Prospect. Robertson's men on the other hand suffered heavy casualties as they fell back towards O'Neill's farm and then made a dash for the base camp. Captain Robertson's report of the episode was said to have made fiery reading. It was judiciously suppressed by the War Office.

*

A word must be interpolated here about the way the situation on Majuba that Sunday had looked to the troops left behind at Mount Prospect. The morning had passed very pleasantly in the camp. We read that the officers there had gathered together to purr over the General's first confident flag signals from Majuba. No one conceived that the Boers might attempt the capture of the hill, let alone succeed. The envious soldiers watched their friends strolling about its summit, and were certain they had won the campaign with a single blow. One of the officers in the camp remembered, when the firing from the hill became heavy, how he and his friends were 'laughing as we sat in our mess tent and saying we wished we were up there potting "Pinheads" as they came up the hill.'[1] Only about 1 p.m. when the first forerunners of defeat were seen scrambling down its slopes, did an uneasy feeling seize Mount Prospect that things might be going badly with Colley on the summit. Incredulity turned to apprehension as the magnitude of the disaster became revealed through the officers' binoculars. All available troops were hurriedly called to arms, and advanced in a skirmishing line to cover the rout of what remained of the Majuba task force, while the guns were galloped forward for a thousand yards to open fire on the advancing Boers. But that day nothing seemed to go right on the British side; the shells fell short, inflicting casualties on the fleeing redcoats and scarcely troubled the enemy. Very soon fugitives from the debacle began to stagger into camp; one of them was shouting that 'it had taken him 5 b . . .y hours to get up Majuba, but he only touched the ground 5 b...y times on the way down.'[1] They were unnerved by their ghastly experience, and exhausted by their flight. Their panic communicated itself immediately to the soldiers in Mount Prospect, some of whom began to make a bolt for the distant safety of Newcastle. One hard drive by Joubert then would probably have enveloped the British camp, and laid all Natal open to invasion. But it was never made: torrential rain began to fall. The soldiers 'fled the camp' explained one of the advancing burghers, 'when they saw their mates coming down the mountain. A plan was suggested by the horsemen to storm the camp but,' as he goes on, 'it was as if the Lord said "thus far and no farther", for at that very moment a thick mist descended in seconds so that one could hardly see ten feet ahead. It was as if the heavens were sorry for the evil deeds of humanity.'[2] It seemed to the burghers that their 'Great General' had suddenly withdrawn his support.

Bad weather may have saved Mount Prospect from annihilation, but it did not prevent the camp from becoming a miserably unhappy place of rumour and gathering recrimination during the next four days. Every report that came in was exaggerated or distorted, while one of the staff officers did not improve morale by insisting that 'the Boers were coming down to attack the camp disguised in the 92nd's kilts and the 58th's redcoats'.[3] 'Some terribly fallacious accounts of the fight are flying about camp and finding credence,' telegraphed one troubled journalist: 'men even who were present advance statements so utterly at variance with what we know to have occurred, that great care is necessary in committing anything to paper.'[4] Different men saw the ordeal they had been through in different ways; portentous explanations, excuses, and harsh recriminations were bandied about between the various units. Private soldiers blamed the officers for bad leadership; officers denounced the men for cowardice. Each regiment insisted that other units 'ran first'. One officer was accused of touching off the panic with a premature order to retire. For four full days the corrosive wrangles continued. Only on the 4th March did morale in Mount Prospect take an upward turn when a soldier on a lathered horse rode into the camp—General Sir Evelyn Wood, V.C. With him he carried an unfamiliar air of resolution, and his mind was brim-full of plans to reverse the verdict of Majuba. And there was a quality in him that fired the spirits of the flagging men. Despondency turned to confidence. Discipline was restored. Morale was fortified. A great curiosity about their new commander seized the soldiers. Their eyes shone more brightly now. They snapped to attention, and hands went up smartly to clean white helmets when Sir Evelyn appeared; and they spun on their heels to watch him ride out on reconnaissance. The redcoats of the Natal Field Force were themselves again, and anxious to whip the Boers.

*

One must pause here again for a moment and go back to consider the experiences of the survivors on the summit of Majuba during the early afternoon of the 27th February immediately following the British rout. The Highlanders on Macdonald's Kopje had been the last to submit; Macdonald himself was taken prisoner after finishing up fighting 'with his bare fists'.[1] For fifty minutes or more afterwards the burghers stood on the shoulder of the plateau shooting the fugitives as they broke cover down its slopes. Carter, who hid for some time in a small cave, remembered listening to the Boers giving an occasional 'exulting shout, sometimes a sudden exclamation, followed by the discharge of a dozen rifles as they got view of a straggler.'[2] At last, about two o'clock that afternoon, tired of the sport, and perhaps stirred a little with regret at the slaughter, the burghers put down their guns, Franz Joubert's commando moved off, and the roar of battle died away. It was replaced by an insistent crying of the wounded. 'It was a terrible thing to view a battlefield,' a horrified young burgher wrote to his father a few days later. 'The mountain was covered with dead, dying and wounded men, and it was impossible to describe the moaning and groaning, the praying, the shouting, the demands for drinks of water and gin, to see the Doctor cut, the moving of the wounded and the gathering of weapons and ammunition.'[1]

When the shooting was over, the summit at first was crowded with Boers. Hamilton, a bewildered captive now, estimated their number at 1,200, but this as it turned out was a gross exaggeration. Some of the younger burghers were still brash and trigger-happy. Dr. Mahon, the surviving surgeon, even had difficulty in preventing them from shooting the dying Romilly. But most English accounts stress the kindness of the burghers. It was characteristic of Commandant-General Joubert (who had startled everyone by riding his pony up the hill at the end of the engagement) to return Lieutenant Hector Macdonald's sword to him, with a shy 'a brave man and his sword should not be separated'.[2] 'There was no boasting, or bragging, or exultation at their victory,'[3] one journalist on the plateau reported after the battle, while another found the Boers 'everywhere exceedingly civil'.[4] It was little wonder that some of the captured soldiers were unable to restrain themselves from admitting their admiration for the victors' splendid achievement. 'We are the mountain Scots,' one private of the 92nd was heard informing a heavily bearded Boer, 'but the Boers are the mountain devils.'[5] Hamilton, after becoming involved in an argument with Joubert about the ethics of the war, came to the conclusion that 'the Boers were not bad fellows', but rather a 'homely sort of people'.[6] With other walking wounded he was allowed to return to the British camp unmolested. Several soldiers' accounts confirm that after the battle their captors' most usual question was, 'why do you fight us on Sunday?',[7] and that they ascribed their victory to an affronted 'God of Battles'.[8] Carter was startled by being asked this curious question: 'now do you English say we are cowards?'[9] and tells us how amused the Boers were to find that, despite the close range at which the engagement had been fought, the soldiers' rifles they picked up were usually sighted at 400 yards.

But if the English were surprised at the unaffected 'homeliness' of their enemies, they were also shocked by their penchant for looting. Cameron, after being taken prisoner, says he was 'promptly divested by my captors of spurs, belt, and some money'.[1] Wright was flabbergasted after surrendering, because the Boers 'immediately rushed at us and began dragging our belts off'[2], and he was not pleased to be relieved of a valuable watch at gun point. Carter was surprised to find that the Boers had removed the shoes from General Colley's dead body and 'even the buttons off his coat'.[3] Hamilton, when he recovered consciousness after being wounded, 'found two small Boers, aged about fourteen, but fully accoutred with rifle and cartridge belts, rolling me over and removing my belts, sword, haversack, etc.'[4] One of the journalists recalled his own captor as being 'very fat, and very much overloaded with rifles, bayonets and cartridge-pouches stuffed full!'[5] But it was the Highlanders' sporrans that were particularly prized as battle trophies; one officer after being deprived of his did not obtain much comfort from the assurance that it would be accorded 'the place of honour' in his new acquaintance's household.[6]

Looking back on it afterwards, the other most vivid recollection of the British survivors on Majuba was of the grisly piles of corpses lying about the plateau. A Scottish officer spoke of 'the horrid sight' of 'a long row of dead men—some forty or fifty of them'[7]—crowded behind the ridge where the last rally had been made, and it was worse at the edge of the hill where he found 'the grass was a mass of blood and brains, and was red all over'. Some among the prisoners, however, were more affected by the agony of the wounded men who nearly all had to be left out in the open during the night that followed the battle. Carter thought their suffering 'something indescribable'[8] and an idea of the ordeal they endured frets through the words of a terse professional report submitted by Dr. Mahon afterwards when he states: 'it now commenced to rain heavily, and continued to do so without intermission during the whole night, which much aggravated the sufferings of the wounded. It also became bitterly cold towards morning. The darkness also was so intense that it was almost impossible to attempt to alleviate the sufferings of the wounded without stumbling over them. We had neither lantern or matches.'[1]

Next morning the Boers allowed a British burial party to ascend the hill. Seventy-five of the bodies found on the plateau were interred in 'three layers' close to the Aid Post, and Captain Maude's was placed separately beside them. He is the only officer to rest on the summit today. Then the corpses littering the hillside were buried where they lay. The body of General Colley was carried by a party of prisoners down to the enemy camp with every mark of respect, and a few days afterwards it was handed over to the British for burial.

Back in their wagon laagers on the evening of the battle, the burghers exploded with joy and thanksgiving. When peace negotiations were initiated a few days later, they gave themselves up to that serene relaxation which for them was the crowning reward of victory. 'Look,' remarked the Mrs. de Jager who had first warned Commandant-General Joubert of his danger, when she approached his men revelling in their well earned repose, 'the nation is resting after its struggle.' Later on, when a township was laid out near by to commemorate the victory, it seemed perfectly natural to name it 'Volksrust' —the peoples' rest.

Post Mortem

On the Monday morning after the battle, the newsboys in Trafalgar Square and the Strand were shouting out that General Colley's army in Natal had suffered another ignominious defeat. London—and then the whole country—was aghast at the news; the sense of gloom deepened when subsequent cables announced that Colley himself had fallen on the field of battle. In those days Generals' lives were considered sacrosanct; convention accorded them safety and respect even in defeat, and it was unprecedented for a British Commander to be shot down in cold blood. Yet the nation's grief was assuaged to some extent by the thought that Colley's death had been a valiant one which had become him very well, and his name was added sadly but proudly to the long list of Victorian heroes who had fallen in the cause of Empire. It came then as a renewed shock when the country began to hear spreading rumours to the effect that the General had not fallen to an enemy bullet, but, after being abandoned by his men, had committed suicide in despair. The story originated from the young soldier of the 58th who stumbled into Mount Prospect after the battle crying out that Colley 'was dead, lying on his back with a bullet through his head, and his revolver, with one barrel empty, lying beside him'.[1] The rumour was fostered when news leaked out about the appearance of the mortal wound, which made it clear that Colley had been shot at very short range; certainly many of the officers of the Natal Field Force, refusing to believe that the Boers would kill a helpless man in cold blood at such close quarters, soon began to mutter among themselves that their dispirited Commander had preferred suicide to facing inevitable censure, not only for losing the battle but for having initiated it. Froude, the historian, was one of those convinced that this was what had happened, and he proceeded to give 'currency to the view that the bullet that killed the General did not come from a Boer rifle—in other words that he fell by his own hand'.

It was a canard that was hardly ever publicly debated in military circles, yet rarely forgotten in private by those concerned. And it was almost certainly untrue. All the available evidence points to Colley having been shot by the Boers. To win credit for themselves after the battle, an extraordinary number of burghers in fact claimed to have fired the fatal shot, but the account given by one of them named Van Royen bears the ring of truth. 'One of the Rooi-baadjies', he recorded later, 'regularly stuck his head out from behind a boulder and shouted out instructions,' so, he goes on to say, he 'fired and hit General Colley in the head.'[2] The Westley-Richards rifle Van Royen used in the battle is still treasured by his descendants.

*

Later, when every aspect of the Battle of Majuba had been scrutinised and discussed, several controversial points besides the manner of Colley's death emerged which were not clearly answered at the time. Did General Colley intend to take guns with him up Majuba? Were the British soldiers engaged there of such poor quality that they broke before they were beaten? Were they so short of ammunition during the battle that, as one report maintained, they were reduced to keeping 'the Boers at a distance by throwing meat tins, stones, etc., at them?'[1] And did Colley act in bad faith when he made an aggressive move during the course of armistice negotiations?

There was much argument about all these points; some of them can be answered more explicitly now than was possible then. Consider the matter of Colley's guns first: Vibart, Colley's senior artillery officer, tells us that the General sent for him some time before undertaking the operation, to enquire whether transport could be improvised to carry mountain guns up Majuba. Vibart goes on to say that he suggested employing *cacolets*, the saddle-shaped stretchers used at the time to carry wounded; but the Principal Medical Officer in the camp flatly refused to lend him any for the purpose, and the project was then utterly dropped.[2] This evidence is conclusive enough: clearly no guns accompanied Colley's movement. Both Norris-Newman and Aylward were wrong when they reported later that the General started off on his night march accompanied by two guns, but was obliged to leave them at the bottom of the hill. Their statements were so similarly worded as to suggest they were derived from a common source, and probably from one which had confused the guns moved out of camp next day to cover the British retreat with those supposed to have accompanied Colley's column.

Turning to the quality of the troops engaged at Majuba, Colonel Stewart, who was fortunate to survive, clearly believed it was poor, for he attributed the disaster to 'the fact that the efforts of the officers were fruitless to check the demoralisation'[3] which followed the enemy advance. But the Gordon Highlanders were the very cream of the British army, noted for their marksmanship, and battle-hardened in Afghanistan. The other regiments admittedly had been badly shaken at Laing's Nek and

Ingogo, but Colley himself had found no fault with them: 'no soldiers could possibly fight more steadily', he had said, 'than the men of the 58th and 60th have done in these two engagements.'[1] It is fair to conclude that, in the same circumstances, any other troops in the British army would have behaved as Colley's men did at Majuba. They were utterly bewildered by the Boers' tactical skill, and demoralised by their fire-power, while their General's own poor leadership had caused them for the time being to lose that fierce refusal to recognise defeat which had become traditional to the British army.

This brings us to the frequently repeated assertion that the soldiers were beaten off Majuba because they ran out of ammunition. The story originated with *The Times* report that a 'handful of Highlanders was the last to leave the hill, and remained there throwing down stones on the Boers. . . .'[2] and it was embellished when the *Natal Mercury* informed its readers that not only were the troops outnumbered thirty to one but had 'exhausted their ammunition'. There is little reliable evidence, however, to support these statements,* and much to refute them. Commandant Ferreira, for instance, in his dispatch after the battle wrote: 'I can assure you with great certainty that near every English soldier forty to seventy rounds was found.'[3]

Whether Colley was ethically correct in acting offensively while his armistice proposal was being considered, will always be a subject for debate and argument. Although he can perhaps be censured on moral grounds for doing so, there is no doubt that technically he could have justified his action. For had the General lived he would have defended himself by pointing out that he had clearly warned President Brand, who was in close touch with the Transvaal leaders, that he would not allow any negotiations to prevent those military moves he considered necessary for the safety of his own troops and the besieged garrisons. He would have argued too that, after he had

---

* Though Carter (quoted in Norris-Newman, p. 203) writes, 'The stand made at this last stage lasted perhaps ten minutes, and then our men fell short of ammunition' (just before the ridge was abandoned).

offered them a truce, the enemy had continued to send out fighting patrols and had fortified a position in Natal which was irrefutably British territory whatever they may have considered the status of the Transvaal to be. Finally General Colley would have emphasised that the forty-eight-hour period he had allowed the Boers to reply to his offer of an armistice had long since expired when he occupied Majuba, and he could hardly be expected to guess that this was due to Kruger's loss of contact with his fighting General. But Colley in his grave was unable to defend himself, and so about his memory even now there clings a faint unfair suggestion that he was an unprincipled soldier who deserved what he got.

*

After the dust from the storm of controversy occasioned by the battle on Majuba had settled, one fact became crystal clear: public opinion was united in denouncing General Colley as the sole author of the catastrophe. Great Britain needed a scape-goat, and what could be more suitable than a dead commander who could not answer back? To understand the nation's feelings about what someone termed Colley's 'want of military capacity', we cannot do better than follow the criticisms of the Hon. J. S. Napier, an eyewitness who made a careful study of the action. 'The disaster', he stated, 'was the result of a series of inexcusable blunders in the art and practice of war. In the first place, there was nothing to gain and everything to lose by premature action. There was no question of the enemy being reinforced, taking the offensive, or even shifting their position; while on the other hand, General Colley's strength might have been doubled within twenty-four hours' notice by moving up troops from Newcastle.' He goes on: 'General Colley staked his all in occupying a position the extent and nature of which were unknown to him, while its distance from Laing's Nek deprived it of any value, it being out of rifle range of the Boer lines. The General had neglected to provide himself with mule guns. . . . As it was, General Colley, after a hard and exhausting night march, found himself in an untenable position, with a handful of men composed of detachments of four distinct corps. He had actually lost his supports and separated himself from his reserve ammunition. When day came no systematic steps were taken either to hold the hill or effect a retreat, although he had four or five hours of daylight before an attack commenced.'[1] It was an accurate and damning analysis.

But if General Colley cannot be exonerated from most of the blame for the disaster on Majuba Hill, then beside him in the dock must stand his own complacent military superiors, as well as the members of Gladstone's vacillating Government. For the Cabinet had asked him to attempt too much with the resources at his disposal, and then had failed to support him whole-heartedly; it had even deceived him regarding its real intentions. The senior officers who administered the British army were still more culpable. They had sent infantry into action dressed conspicuously in pipe clayed helmets and red tunics with polished buttons; they had preferred to teach their soldiers parade-ground precision rather than marksmanship, so that some of the most wretched shots in the world were pitted in South Africa against its best; worse still, their passionate devotion to the deadly routine of army life had killed the living spirit of tactical enterprise, and had produced commanders who failed disastrously when opposed by determined white men instead of crudely-armed natives.

But the most disturbing feature of the battle on Majuba was not to be revealed for another twenty years: for it turned out then that the British High Command had profited not at all from the lessons that should have been learned there. Although Colley's tactical mistakes had been recognised, endlessly discussed, and unanimously condemned, none of them were really taken to heart. Instead, the British troops who fought the Transvaalers again in 1899 were handled with the same fatuous incompetence as those of 1881. The blunders which had lost the earlier struggle were seen again and again during the Second Boer War—and on a larger and more disastrous scale. Nowhere was this more noticeable than in the battle for that other 'hill of destiny', Spion Kop. The fighting there seemed like a ghastly episode of *déjà vu*, for by the uncanny symmetry of history the events of the earlier battle were re-enacted there feature by feature.

The same crass fumbling by an English commander, who yet somehow still retained the confidence of his men after two badly conducted battles, turned initial success into humiliating defeat. After failing to pierce a Boer entrenched position with a frontal assault, a hilltop which commanded it was seized without loss following a bold night march. The neglect to dig proper trenches and the failure to grasp the tactical significance of the hill's natural defences were then faithfully repeated on Spion Kop. Tactically both battles were lost because of the English troops' poor shooting, and the skilful use the Boers made of cover during a counter-attack. Each action ended with the hill in Boer hands after the English had suffered heavy and absurdly disproportionate casualties. General Buller at Spion Kop, in fact, made every mistake Colley had committed on Majuba. The only difference was that Buller lived to blame them all on someone else. His failure was all the more ironical because Buller had been one of the most scathing of Sir George's critics, and when discussing Colley's inexperience of South Africa's 'infernal hills' had chortled in words whose memory must afterwards have often returned to make him wince: 'he'll climb one of them, but . . . won't understand that the top's no use unless you know which ridge to guard.'[1]

But one is almost glad that General Colley did not survive Majuba. Although he had served his country ill, he emerges from the battle as a figure deserving less of obloquy and censure than of our sympathetic understanding. He had been moulded in a pattern that had suddenly become out of date in 1881; and he had failed to free himself from the bondage of frustrated ambition. Today his failure to subdue rebellion in the Transvaal is a part of history, and his last battle has taken on something of the aura of a myth. For its context now seems to be nearly as far lost in the mist of time as those of Thermopylae and Actium. But the line of schanzes against the skyline that stare across the haunted lowlands of Natal from Laing's Nek have scarcely altered since the burghers built them. They are real enough. The white memorials stand out as starkly against the bare grasslands of Schuin's Hoogte as they did nearly ninety years ago, and the dramatic silhouette of Majuba still towers above the old Transvaal frontier like a grim sepulchre commemorating the men who died upon her.

Today, after scrambling up the steep slopes of Majuba Hill to stand at last breathless on its summit, the visitor is overwhelmed by the immense and brooding silence of the place. The air there is threaded through with the memories of all the young lives thrown away for a cause they did not understand, and which their Government would soon abandon; the very rocks scattered across the plateau seem still to grieve over what they saw that February day of 1881. Yet, as one lingers on the theatrical stage of Majuba's summit, one's sadness slowly becomes tempered by happier thoughts. No views in the world can rival those of southern Africa, and this one from the hill where the soldiers died is perhaps the fairest of them all. Those who are buried here could have asked for no more beautiful resting place. That is the transcendent thought the modern visitor carries away from Majuba Hill.

Part Three

AFTERMATH

The fighting of the First Boer War in fact ended with General Colley's rout on Majuba Hill. But for some time after that *débâcle*, everyone expected it to be renewed on a much larger scale. 'Now we have been defeated', Cameron, one of the war correspondents who was captured on the hill top, briskly informed Commandant-General Joubert, 'the war must go on.' And that was most people's immediate reaction to the disaster. England's military prestige must be re-established at all costs, and at once. For although the engagement had been only a trivial one, it was formidable in the passions it aroused. Queen Victoria, who had already advised Lord Kimberley not to make peace 'before a victory has been won', reflected the national mood in her journal entry of the 6th March, 1881, when she affirmed: 'I do not like peace before we have retrieved our honour';[1] and even the arch-appeaser of the Cabinet, John Bright, after receiving the 'bad news from the Transvaal', confessed in his own diary that they made the 'prospect of peace much further off'.[2]

The War Office reacted promptly and strongly to the crisis. Although England was always short of troops for her Imperial commitments, six infantry battalions and three regiments of cavalry were given orders to sail immediately for South Africa, while Sir Frederick Roberts was appointed to Colley's vacant command. No one had any doubt that the victor of Kandahar with such massive reinforcements would speedily crush the rebels.

And up at Mount Prospect Sir Evelyn Wood was spoiling for another fight—and he was most anxious to have it before Roberts arrived. Now this was the old George Colley situation all over again, except that Sir Evelyn was a rather more

restrained man than his predecessor. As it was, only bad
weather and the General's tardy decision that a soldier's wishes
must in the end be subordinated to those of his Government,
prevented him from setting his own cherished scheme in
motion and turning the Boer line at Laing's Nek with an advance through Wakkerstroom.

But on 4th March, Joubert, at President Brand's instigation,
offered to meet Sir Evelyn in two days' time to arrange an
armistice until Kruger's long-awaited reply from Rustenburg
had been received. Wood was dubious about agreeing and
asked Kimberley for instructions, informing him at the same
time that 'my constant endeavour shall be to carry out the spirit
of your orders; but, considering the disaster we have sustained,
I think the happiest result will be that, after accelerating
successful action, which I hope to fight in about fourteen days,
the Boers should disperse without any guarantee.'[1]

But in the end Wood did meet Joubert on the 6th as had
been suggested; and somewhat cynically and on his own
responsibility he agreed to an eight days' truce. As he pointed
out to London, those eight days would not only allow him time
to complete his military dispositions, but, he gleefully added, he
had persuaded the Boers to allow him to revictual the beleaguered British garrisons during the cease fire. Next day
Kruger's reply to Colley's crucial forty-eight-hour ultimatum
reached Joubert and was at last delivered to Mount Prospect.
It sounded more conciliatory than had been expected, and when
Wood transmitted its contents to London, he must have known
that the Cabinet would grasp at the chance it gave them of
agreeing to a compromise peace. All he could do was attempt
to stiffen the Ministry's resolution. 'Do not imagine I wish to
fight,' he piously assured Kimberley in an accompanying cable,
'but now you have so many troops coming, I recommend
decided though lenient action, and I can, humanly speaking,
promise victory. Colley never engaged more than six companies; I shall use twenty, and two Cavalry regiments in
directions known only to myself, and I undertake to enforce
dispersion.'[2]

But within a week of her first outburst of indignation, England's mood of belligerency had suddenly passed. She had grown bored with the stupid little war against a handful of farmers six thousand miles away, particularly as it was one which her statesmen were now busily assuring everyone had been immoral from the start. For, as Wood had surmised, the Cabinet was inclining towards meeting most of the Trans-vaalers' demands, and was hard at work persuading public opinion of the propriety of doing so. For some days Kimberley had been addressing plaintive telegrams to Mount Prospect, asking what had become of the peace proposals he had asked Colley to pass on to Kruger; then the influential Joseph Chamberlain announced he was 'out and out for negotiations with the Boers,'[1] and made all the progressive heads in parliament shake with indignation at the injustice that had been inflicted on 'a brave little people'. It was a strange attitude to adopt for the future jingo-imperialist who was responsible perhaps more than any other man for crushing the Transvaal twenty years later. As for Mr. Gladstone, he had again become a prey to torturing doubts. The way his mind was working at this time comes out in a minute he wrote to Kimberley in a typical burst of Gladstonian prose: 'Suppose for argument's sake', his polemical pen argued, 'that at the moment when Colley made the unhappy attack on Majuba Hill, there shall turn out to have been decided on, and possibly on its way, a satisfactory or friendly reply from the Boer Government to your telegram? I fear the chances may be against this; but if it prove the case, we could not because we have failed on Satuday night, insist on shedding more blood.'[2]

Only a few days later, the Prime Minister's supposition 'for argument's sake' was seen to be precisely what had actually occurred. Kruger had made his reply, and it was undeniably 'satisfactory': it was even 'friendly', and it crystallised all Mr. Gladstone's hesitations. From the moment that it reached him, the Prime Minister was determined to obtain peace at any price, or at least, at nearly any price. 'Before these military miscarriages', he unburdened himself in another note to a friend, 'we were prepared to treat with the rebels': now, he asked, would it be right to 'offer up a certain number of victims in expiation of the blood that has been shed?'[1] He was certain it would not; every fibre of his being told him that to seek a victory merely to regain prestige was a course unworthy of a Christian democracy, and even more unworthy of a Liberal Government. And so, despite Wood's repetitive cables about 'the happiest result' and his hopes for 'decided though lenient action', the General at Mount Prospect was crisply instructed to prolong the military truce until peace terms could be mutually agreed upon.

Who can say that Gladstone's arguments and decisions were unsound? And who can deny that in one sense they were courageous? For the Prime Minister knew full well he would be accused of adopting a policy of 'scuttle' if he appeased the Boers, and by nobody more sharply than the Queen. He knew too he would be criticised for failing to avenge Colley and the other British dead, as well as for abandoning the loyalists living in the Transvaal and the natives who had trusted the British Government to protect them; above all, he knew he would be denounced for conceding to force what he had refused again and again to mere entreaty. All these charges that would be laid against him might bring his political career to an end, but Gladstone steadfastly pursued the course he believed was the right one; at the very least he could comfort himself with the thought that it would prevent more blood being spilled. And quietening their private misgivings, the other members of the Cabinet gave him their support.

The Liberal ministers, unanimous at last in pusillanimity, now erupted into a volcano of verbiage and cant in an effort to justify themselves; platforms throughout the country rang with well-practised declamations about the 'blood-guiltiness of conducting an unjust war', of 'adopting a generous course', and of 'magnanimity to a brave people'. Yet the feeling grew among the more perspicacious members of the community that the Government's decision not to see the war through was prompted less by 'righting an injustice' than by a degrading fear that the Transvaalers' kinsmen in the Orange Free State and Cape Colony might join the rebels in arms and present too powerful a combination for the British army to subdue in the foreseeable future.

In Natal, obedient to the Government's instructions, Sir Evelyn Wood grudgingly prolonged the military truce with Joubert. The venue of the two men's talks was O'Neill's cottage standing just below Laing's Nek, about midway between the English and Boer positions. It was a small stone building with a corrugated-iron roof hiding in a wooded glade that might have been transported to Africa straight from Gloucestershire. In a room still stinking from the festering wounds of the soldiers who had been nursed there after the battle, the two men drew rickety chairs across mud floors to a plain wooden table and proceeded to hammer out provisional peace terms. Presently they were joined in their arguments by other frock-coated Transvaal delegates, and stiff officers in the Queen's uniform stroking indignant waxed moustaches.

It was not a particularly affable conference. Evelyn Wood was personally opposed to any concessions, and when he had to make some, he left no doubt in any one's mind that he was merely carrying out his Government's distasteful instructions. For his part Kruger, when he eventually arrived at O'Neill's, was unwilling to accept anything but complete independence for his country. The exchanges became so heated one day that the Boer delegates stamped down the cottage steps to prepare an immediate attack on the English camp at Mount Prospect, and as late as the 16th of March a flushed Sir Evelyn assured assembled newspaper correspondents 'we are no nearer peace than ever we were, and unless the Boers moderate their tone, the negotiations will come to nothing'.[1] That same day he repeated his previous conviction to the Government in London that 'the happiest result will be that, after accelerating successful action, which I hope to fight . . . the Boers should disperse without any guarantee'.[2] His advice, however, was airily ignored by Lord Kimberley.

As the talks dragged on, the journalists hanging about outside O'Neill's cottage confessed they were becoming heartily 'tired of these negotiations'. They lost interest in the harassed military gentlemen they watched gesticulating at the cottage windows; they grew bored with the bearded Boer delegates who stalked out on to the little verandah to confer in hoarse whispers with each other. But the rupture which appeared inevitable was prevented by the arrival at the conference of that Solomon of intermediaries, President Brand. Ruffled tempers were soothed by his impartial urbanity, and gradually the armistice negotiations took on a momentum of their own, which was difficult for anyone to halt.

By the 23rd March, both sides had wearily made enough concessions to allow them to keep the truce until such time as a Royal Commission had met to draw up a formal peace treaty.

But both the British and the Boers turned out to be extremely reticent regarding armistice terms they had negotiated at O'Neill's cottage. Joubert was well aware that if his commandos knew some of their clauses they would refuse to disperse, preferring to renew the fight. He, however, had not been called 'slim' without reason. He was certain that once a cease-fire had been agreed upon, Great Britain would never renew the war, and that later on the Transvaalers would have no difficulty in modifying the terms to suit themselves.

When all the scrawly signatures had been affixed in O'Neill's cottage to the long document which closed the First Boer War, and the delegates had trooped outside to stand in an awkward line for a photographer to immortalise the occasion, the burghers—still ignorant of its details—inspanned their wagons and rolled away from the defences they had held so staunchly for nearly three months. 'Now you can have a look at the Nek,' one of them sneered to a member of Wood's staff before he left, and the British soldiers did exactly that. As the last burgher's wagon rattled across the Coldstream into the Transvaal, a crowd of sightseeing redcoats came surging up the road to goggle at the Boer lines before clambering up what was already the legendary hill of Majuba. 'The place stank,' Carter reported gravely of the Laing's Nek position; 'offal, rubbish, filth, and every abomination lay on the surface of the veldt', and he was sure that if the Boers 'had not left the spot very soon, fever or some virulent disease would have done what our force had failed to accomplish'.[1]

Yet even now it seemed that the fighting might begin again. For Wood's restraint and his natural affability, which had charmed the Boer delegates, changed to irascibility when he travelled into the Transvaal and sensed the contempt its people felt for the British whom they had so easily defeated. He first made difficulties about the composition of the Royal Commission, and brusquely rejected Kruger's demand that some Transvaalers should be included among its members. Then he flatly refused to withdraw the British garrison troops from the country until peace terms had been ratified by both Governments, and it was only with great reluctance that he withdrew a face-saving demand that before concluding peace his troops be allowed to march through the Transvaal as though it were a subjugated country. On the 19th April Sir Evelyn became so infuriated by Boer truculence that he seriously advised a stunned Lord Kimberley to break off the truce, and allow him to 'fight it out' again with the burghers back in their original positions. 'I should allow them to reoccupy Nek!' he cabled, 'we are quite ready. This will give a decisive military result, and the happiest result for the country. I guarantee we dislodge them.'[2]

But Joubert found such quixotic military gestures as a renewal of the duel on Laing's Nek a trifle out of date. In any case his commandos had long since dispersed, and he had every intention of preventing Sir Evelyn finding any armed burghers to fight. He was still striving for conciliation: 'We shall not win now,' he explained to Kruger; 'I am in favour of a peaceful settlement'. And he placated Wood's injured feelings by allowing him to effect a sham relief of the Potchefstroom garrison as though it had never surrendered after all.

*

The truce of O'Neill's cottage was eventually ratified in the August of 1881 by the signing of the Convention of Pretoria. Only then were the peace terms publicised, and they were greeted with a roar of disapproval from both the Transvaal and Great Britain. The Convention restored quasi-independence to a reconstituted South African Republic (which was now officially named the Transvaal) subject to a loosely defined suzerainty by the Queen. It also provided for the appointment of a British Resident at Pretoria with powers to exercise general supervision over the country's native population. The Republic's relationships with foreign powers were subjected to Great Britain's approval, and the Crown retained possession of all districts of the Transvaal east of longitude 30°, which were to be administered in the interests of their African residents. Finally England reserved the right to march troops through the Republic in time of war, and insisted on political equality for all white people in the Transvaal, whatever their country of origin.

For Great Britain, the defeated party, these were undeniably favourable terms. The trouble was that no one in the Transvaal had any intention of abiding by them. The burghers were deeply suspicious of the meanings which might be placed on the word 'suzerainty'; not unnaturally they could not reconcile independence with the British Parliament's control of their foreign policy; and they bitterly opposed separation from the fatherland of the eastern part of the country, which comprised the districts of Utrecht, Wakkerstroom, Ermelo, Lydenburg, Barberton and most of the Zoutpansberg.

The new Transvaal Government promptly began a campaign to whittle down the peace terms to its satisfaction, and they were successful sooner than even the most optimistic burghers could have hoped. For with the rising furore of the troubles in Ireland and the Sudan, England had little time to spare for the fresh grievances of the always bothersome Transvaal. And on the third anniversary of Majuba, amid dazed protests from Queen Victoria, Great Britain tacitly dropped most of the offending clauses and signed a new treaty. The Transvaal, by the Convention of London, entirely recovered her *de facto* independence. Majuba had not been fought in vain.

*

It was not surprising that the Boers, who had thus regained their freedom by defeating the *Rooineks* on four separate occasions and at such remarkably small cost, should have believed they were quite capable of checking any further attempt by Great Britain to reassert her paramountcy over South Africa. But they were mistaken.

For fate willed it that after administering the poison of Majuba Hill to Great Britain's Imperial aspirations in the sub-continent, the antidote in turn was almost immediately pre-scribed. Only six weeks after the battle, a young man named Cecil John Rhodes took his seat in the Cape Legislature, and one of the rare souls who revived his countrymen's faith in themselves, began to make his voice heard through the land.

It was a small voice at first, but it was the authentic voice of Victorian Empire. For some time, however, the initiative still rested with Paul Kruger. Majuba day was celebrated each year with increasing arrogance in his Republic. The President chose to disregard even the terms he himself had supported in the Conventions of Pretoria and London. He plainly aspired now to an Afrikaner hegemony of South Africa. Political rights were largely denied in the Transvaal to residents not of Boer descent. The Republic's boundaries, fixed by treaty, were unilaterally expanded by the annexation of 'The New Republic' carved out of Zululand by a handful of venturesome burghers, and by the virtual proclamation of Goshen and Stellaland as Boer Protectorates. The old conceit that the Boers were God's Elect was fostered when the wealth which had been so carefully concealed by nature during the British occupation, was revealed to the 'chosen people' in 1886. That revelation could not have been more opportune; the Boer Republic by then was already returning to the chaos and bankruptcy which had led Shepstone to proclaim the annexation in 1877. But when the vast gold reef of the Rand was opened up, Kruger suddenly found himself possessed of funds to win support for his chauvinistic policy, and (what was more important) to buy modern arms. Relations with London steadily deteriorated. The Afrikaner Bond was encouraged to foment nationalism among the Boers living in the British South African colonies; and the President negotiated several secret treaties with foreign powers, which, despite his previous assurances, were plainly directed against the interests of Great Britain. Responsibility for the rising storm was by no means one-sided. With the discovery of such fabulous wealth within her borders, the Transvaal changed suddenly from an insolvent republic into the most desirable piece of real estate on earth. Imperial Britain coveted the country which Gladstone had so lightly abandoned in 1881, and Majuba Hill became for her not only a synonym for humiliation and defeat, but a reminder of the riches which might have been hers. Persuasion and threats failed to shift Kruger from his intransigent attitude on British rights in the Transvaal. A mad filibustering raid led by Dr. Jameson to regain the country was given at least some official support, but was ignominiously defeated. And as the exuberant Empire nearing the high noon of her power scanned the horizon for new vistas of expansion, her gaze froze again and again on the repugnant shape of Majuba.

It had seemed a trivial enough affair in 1881; as battles went the fight on Majuba had been no more than a skirmish. But in its story were strangely gathered all the emotional ingredients of a drama; and as time unfolded the battle was invested with a military significance it never possessed, and the hill took on a new dimension of its own. The British people came to believe with Cecil Rhodes that only by avenging Majuba could they fulfil their 'Manifest Destiny'. The memory of Colley's defeat rankled increasingly in their minds, and became one of the prime motives which drove their Empire to war against the Transvaal for a second time in 1899.

Nor was it ever far away from the thoughts of all the combatants engaged in that second war. The Queen's soldiers went into action shouting, 'remember Majuba': the Boers drew resilience from its memory; and when General Cronje, who all those years before had invited the malcontents to release Bezuidenhout's wagon at Potschefstroom, was obliged to surrender to Lord Roberts at Paardeberg on the nineteenth anniversary of the battle, he did so with a bitter 'you have even taken our Majuba day away from us'.

In 1902, when the last commandos submitted to the massive British armies deployed against them, it seemed that events had turned full circle and Majuba had been truly avenged. But the eerie 'hill of destiny' continued to throw its incalculable shadow across history. If for the British it had ceased to symbolise humiliation, now it took on new status for the Boers. To them the battle on its summit became a legend, a living Afrikaner legend, a legend every bit as valid as that of the Great Trek. Remembrance of Joubert's old victory inspired them to accomplish the impossible, and the Boer people rose above the misery of 1902 to win the peace that followed. Afrikaner nationalism had always crystallised round the problem of Transvaal independence, and now the memory of their fathers' fight on the 'hill of doves', which once before had regained that freedom, became the touchstone of their determination to win independence back again. The Great Trek was honoured by them a little nostalgically as a most splendid epic of their folk history, but they recognised it had not strengthened, but rather dispersed, their nation. For it had slackened the holy bonds of Afrikanerdom by dividing them into a homely north and genteel south. But this other epic of Majuba had catalysed their patriotism, had served to unite them as a people. The myth which had grown up around that chance victory helped to create the vision of a single Afrikaner nation with a shared sentiment and a common destiny.

The pride in their kinsmen's feat on Majuba Hill made the burghers of the Cape and Free State aware of the ties of blood which joined them to the Transvaalers. All of them now yearned to preserve their joint heritage. They revived old grievances and built them up into a folk saga to cement their new-found group awareness. The taal was resurrected and made into a living language. A version of the past, which the outside world considered distorted, was projected into the future (and especially into the political future) so that new generations of white South Africans could not prevent themselves becoming captives of their own fable. Inevitably they adopted a pattern of life which seemed anachronistic to less colour-conscious nations; and yet, somehow, they drew strength from the ostracism they in consequence endured.

Lord Carnarvon's old dream of a federated South Africa had been revived again by the expanding legend of Majuba, but this time it appeared in an Afrikaner idiom, and was dominated by the opulent Transvaal. The vision of 'one nation stretching from Simon's Bay to the Zambezi' came closer to realisation, but over it was now arraigned not the Union Jack but the *vierkleur* which Smit's burghers had hoisted so long before on the summit of Macdonald's Kopje.

Who now can doubt that but for the victory on Majuba, South Africa would have been absorbed into the British way of life, or that the inevitable national unity of its white people would have been built on more liberal foundations? And who can deny that if General Colley had possessed one ounce of tactical flare, Carnarvon's vision rather than Kruger's would have been realised in the subcontinent, and the lives of millions of people today cast in different moulds?

APPENDIX I

Although the number of men who fought on Majuba Hill barely exceeded eight hundred, some of them were later to become well known to the world.

Commandant-General Joubert grew into a political rival to Paul Kruger in the Transvaal Republic, and twice unsuccessfully contested the Presidency with him. On the outbreak of the second South African war he assumed command of the Boer forces and presided over their early successes. He died in March, 1900, after a short illness, and rests now in an impressive tomb not far from the scene of his triumph on Majuba. Not only his own countrymen, but his enemies, mourned this rough good-humoured, working soldier; Rudyard Kipling who was not much given to lauding the adversaries of his country, yet composed a sonnet to the Boer Commander's chivalry in war:

> With those that bred, with those that loosed the strife
> He had no part, whose hands were clear of gain;
> But subtle, strong and stubborn, gave his life,
> To a lost cause, and knew the gift was vain.[1]

Colonel Stewart who had gained very little repute from the Battle of Majuba, only four years later distinguished himself by leading his troops to victory at Abu Klea during the march to relieve Khartoum. He was mortally wounded next day: this had a profound influence on history, for his command passed to Sir Charles Wilson, whose subsequent dilatory tactics were blamed at the time for General Gordon's death.

Ian Hamilton's wound at Majuba left him with a permanently crippled arm, but this did not prevent his rising to the top of his profession. In some ways his charm, aestheticism and imagination remind us of his old Commander, General Colley.

He was a man with many friends, one of whom, Andrew Lang, immortalised his gallantry on 'the Shameful Hill' of Majuba (in a way that must have made his hero squirm) with:

> To you, who know the force of war,
> You, that for England wander far,
> You, that have seen the Ghazis fly
> From English lads not born to die;
> You, that have lain where, deadly chill,
> The mist crept o'er the Shameful Hill;
> You that have conquered, mile by mile,
> The currents of unfriendly Nile,
> And cheered the March, and eased the strain
> When politics made valour vain,
> Ian, to you, from banks of Ken,
> We send our lays of Englishmen!

Hamilton was always convinced that a bayonet attack would have won the day at Majuba, and years later when the Boers penetrated the perimeter of Ladysmith, he remembered the lesson and drove them out with a counter-attack which saved the town.

In 1915 Sir Ian Hamilton led the disastrous expedition to Gallipoli, where he left his military but not his chivalrous reputation. He died as recently as 1947.

Among the burghers who climbed the eastern face of Majuba Hill with Ferreira in 1881 was a celebrated hunter named Christiaan de Wet. At Nicholson's Nek during the Second Boer War he led a commando to a victory whose features bore so curious a resemblance to the earlier triumph that it became known as 'Little Majuba'. De Wet later became the most famous of all the Boer guerrilla leaders, evading every attempt to capture him. Indeed his renown so impressed London Society that it inspired one of King Edward's most applauded *bon mots*: talking of a notorious match-making mother he chortled, 'they ought to set her to catch de Wet'. General De Wet's continued hatred for the British made him lead a rebellion against the South African Government when the Great War of 1914 broke out. He was quickly captured and found guilty of high treason, but after a short term in prison, was released.

Lieutenant Hector Macdonald gained notoriety of a different kind at the end of his life. He had been twenty-nine when he defended the western 'breast' of Majuba against Smit's burghers, and he was already famous as one of the few rankers in the British army who had been commissioned as an officer. His reputation and status continued to progress. Colonel Macdonald became a lion of society after distinguished service at Omdurman and during the Second Boer War; he was knighted, promoted Major-General, and appointed A.D.C. to his Sovereign. In his homeland, 'fighting Mac' was honoured as the greatest Scottish soldier since Wallace. But his fabulous career ended when 'very grave charges' concerned with homosexual affairs were brought against him. Macdonald was sent home from his command in Ceylon. He was granted an audience with King Edward, who was rumoured to have suggested that only suicide would avert the public scandal of a court martial. A few days later, in a small bedroom of the Regina Hotel in Paris, one of the few eyewitnesses of General Colley's death on the summit of Majuba put his own revolver to his ear, and pulled the trigger.

APPENDIX II

The Transvaal Garrisons

Nothing is more remarkable in the story of the First Anglo-Boer War than the way Victorian England sought solace from the sad and terrible disasters that had overcome Colley's troops by glamorising the part the soldiers of the besieged garrisons played during that struggle. After all, six of the seven garrisons had successfully withstood three months siege, and the seventh had only been tricked into surrender after the armistice had been initiated. An engaging tableau of valour and endurance emerged from the vision the public conjured up. That tableau was utterly false. The hard fact is that in nearly every case the garrisons were defended with a depressing lack of spirit, while the sieges were conducted with wild incompetence and irresolution. The garrisons occupied the attention of only a small proportion of the Boer forces, and they did extremely little to ease Colley's task of crushing the Transvaal rebellion.

At Pretoria, on the outbreak of war, nearly 2,000 troops and armed volunteers (who had the misfortune to be commanded by Colonel Bellairs) abandoned the town and took refuge in the convent, gaol and sundry nearby earthworks. They were opposed by 600 burghers who were content to contain the garrison by sitting in comfortable laagers six or more miles away. Admittedly Bellairs conducted three sorties into the no-man's-land which separated the adversaries: the first was ineffectual, and the other two both ended in furious recriminations and ignominious withdrawals. The British lost 16 killed and 37 wounded during the siege; the Boer casualties amounted to 6 killed and 5 wounded. The investment was dignified by a strike by the garrison's medical men for higher pay; while the announcement of peace was enlivened by two separate burnings of Gladstone's effigy; and a subsequent inspection of the garrison by Sir Evelyn Wood was marred by shouts of 'bunkum' from the ranks.

The investment of Potchefstroom was a more serious affair. The earthworks hastily erected by the British just outside the town covered an area of only twenty-five yards square, and into them were crowded 140 soldiers and about an equal number of civilians. Potchefstroom's garrison was the only one of the seven which was inadequately provisioned; during the siege it lost 31 dead and 54 wounded. The Boers engaged 400 men during the siege; they were commanded by Piet Cronje who suppressed news of the negotiations at O'Neill's cottage and accepted the garrison's surrender on the 21st March 1881. In view of this 'duplicity' Sir Evelyn Wood, before he signed the armistice which ended the war, insisted that the capitulation be 'cancelled', the garrison's captured guns delivered to him, and a token reoccupation of the fort effected by British troops.

Sixty soldiers, nine volunteers, and one English lady saw the war out from an earthen fort at Lydenburg with the loss of three men killed. At Wakkerstroom, within ear-shot of the battles round Laing's Nek, another seventy soldiers and loyalists held out against a varying number of burghers without much difficulty, only losing two men during the siege. A similar number of soldiers at Rustenburg endured an equally uneventful investment, but this garrison made an unexpected contribution to the drama of Majuba by obliging Paul Kruger to pay a morale-raising visit to their besiegers, which made it impossible for him to reply quickly to Colley's forty-eight-hour ultimatum.

The defence of Standerton was conducted by 420 men with more spirit than was shown in any of the other garrisons; indeed their antics remind one of those of Baden-Powell's men during the Second Boer War siege of Mafeking. They were opposed by a force of burghers variously estimated at between 250 and 1,200. The British losses at Standerton were 5 killed and 9 wounded.

The sixty soldiers of the most northerly British garrison in the Transvaal found themselves cooped up at Marabastad in an earthwork scarcely larger than a tennis court, and there they were joined by 35 loyalist civilians whom a happy coincidence had brought into the district to attend the first Zoutpansberg races on the day hostilities commenced. During the 105-day siege that followed, the Boers discovered an old ship's carronade which they brought into action against the fort, but they were really far more interested in the remarkable ashlar chimney which stood three miles away at the abandoned Eersteling mine where the first payable gold strike in the Transvaal had been made. This high chimney-stack had come to represent to them the strength and durability of the Victorian Empire; indeed they said that when it fell so would the British power in southern Africa. One day, becoming tired of the interminable siege, the Boers took time off from their military duties, yoked a double team of oxen to the chimney and tried to pull it down. They failed. In 1967 the chimney is still standing at Eersteling, splendidly isolated and loftily conscious that it won the only British success in a disastrous war.

BIBLIOGRAPHY

The following books and articles (and their abbreviations where appropriate) are those referred to in the references notes.

Bellairs, Lady Blanche: *The Transvaal War 1880–1*, Blackwood, 1885.

B. & R. = Blanch, H. J. and Rywell, M.: *English Guns and Gun Makers*, Pioneer Press, Harriman, Tennessee, 1956.

Bond, B. *History Today*, XV, 7, 1965.

BBB = British Blue Book C-2950.

B = Butler, Sir W. F.: *The Life of Sir George Pomeroy Colley*, John Murray, 1899.

C = Carter, Thomas Fortescue: *A Narrative of the Boer War*, Cape Town, Juta, 1896.

Coupland, R.: *Zulu Battlepiece*, Collins, 1948.

Cromb, James: *The Story of Majuba Hill: a tale of Highland heroism told by officers of the 92nd Regiment*, 2nd ed. Glasgow, David Bryce, 1899.

Garvin, J. L.: *The Life of Joseph Chamberlain*, Vol. I, Macmillan, 1932.

Haggard, Sir Henry Rider: *The Last Boer War*, Kegan Paul, 1900.

Ham = Hamilton, Sir Ian; *Listening for the Drums*, Faber, 1944.

Hendry, Hamish: *Majuba, Bronkerspruit, Ingogo, Lang's Nek, and Krugersdorp*, Grant Richards, 1900.

Holt, E.: *The Boer War*, Putnam, 1958.

I-M = Iwan-Müller, E. B.: *Lord Milner and South Africa*, Heinemann, 1902.

Kruger, S. J. P.: *The Memoirs of Paul Kruger*, Fisher Unwin, 1902.

Marling, Sir Percival: *Rifleman and Hussar*, John Murray, cheap ed., 1935.

Montgomery, John: *Toll for the Brave*, Max Parrish, 1963.

Morley, J.: *The Life of William Ewart Gladstone*, Vol. III, Macmillan, 1903.

Napier, Lord: *Letters of*, Jarrold, Norwich, 1936.

Nathan, M.: *Paul Kruger,* Knox Publishing House, Durban, 5th ed., 1946.

N–N = Newman, Charles L. Norris-: *With the Boers in the Transvaal and Orange Free State in 1880–1,* Allen, 1882.

S–C = *Staats Courant,* 'Der Zuid-Afrikaansche Republiek', March 16th 1881.

Trevelyan, G. M.: *The Life of John Bright,* Constable, 1913.

Tylden, G.: *Society of Army Historical Research Journal,* 1957.

Vulliamy, C. E.: *Outlanders,* Jonathan Cape, 1938.

Victoria, Queen: *The Letters of,* Second series, Vol. III, John Murray, 1928.

Walker, E. A.: *A History of Southern Africa,* 3rd ed., Longmans, Green, 1957.

Wood, Sir Evelyn: *From Midshipman to Field-Marshal,* cheap ed., Methuen, 1912.

REFERENCES

PAGE	REF. NO.	SOURCE	PAGE	REF. NO.	SOURCE
8	1	*Encyc. Brit.* 1962, Vol. 22, p. 420	4		B. 268
			38	1	B. 283
11	1	Coupland. 28		2	B. 282
12	1	Vulliamy. 23	40	1	Cromb. 49
	2	N–N. 81	41	1	Walker. 383
13	1	Walker. 363	43	1	Vulliamy. 75
14	1	I–M. 148		2	Vulliamy. 68
15	1	I–M. 162	48	1	B. 291
16	1	Kruger. 154		2	N–N. 151
	2	N–N. 194	50	1	B. & R. 82
17	1	C. 80		2	N–N. 344
19	1	Coupland. 130		3	Marling. 41
	2	Vulliamy. 51.	51	1	Morley. 34
20	1	I–M. 233 : C. 78	52	1	Wood. 309
	2	Morley. III. 26		2	B. 322
21	1	I–M. 237, 247	53	1	Wood. 313
	2	C. 97	54	1	B. 294
22	1	B. 265		2	B. 313
24	1	B. 268 (letter 11 Dec. from Lanyon.)	56	1	Marling. 47
			58	1	C. 209
	2	B. 268.	59	1	N–N. 160
26	1	N–N. 299		2	C. 212
	2	N–N. 336		3	C. 216
27	1	N–N. 123	60	1	B. 334
	2	N–N. 337		2	B. 309
	3	N–N. 121	61	1	Bellairs. 389
	4	Holt. 22	62	1	C. 229
28	1	C. 132		2	C. 260
	2	N–N. 124	63	1	B. 334
	3	B. 269		2	B. 340
29	1	B. 277		3	N–N. 353
31	1	Vulliamy. 56	64	1	B. 338
32	1	B. 50		2	B. 338
33	1	B. 126		3	B. 339
	2	B. 233		4	B. 339
34	1	B. 235	65	1	N–N. 353
	2	B. 238		2	N–N. 353
35	1	B. 148	65	3	N–N. 354
	2	B. 110		4	B. 343
	3	Holt. 23	66	1	C. 344/5
36	1	B. 255		2	B. 344
	2	B. 275		3	C. 344/5
	3	B. 257	67	1	C. 231

PAGE	REF. NO.	SOURCE	PAGE	REF. NO.	SOURCE
	2	C. 231, B. 344	88	1	Cromb. 18
	3	N–N. 352		2	C. 307
70	1	B. 361	89	1	C. 300
	2	Vulliamy. 70		2	C. 300
71	1	Montgomery. 36		3	Ham. 134
	2	Vulliamy, 71		4	Nathan. 166
	3	Haggard, 155.	91	1	C. 300
72	1	Vulliamy. 71		2	B. 386
	2	B. 348	92	1	B. 386
	3	Cromb. 39		2	B. 387
73	1	Marling. 52		3	C. 260
	2	C. 253		4	B. & R. 83
75	1	C. 253	93	1	Cromb. 38
76	1	B. 367	95	1	BBB.
77	1	B. 369		2	B. 391
78	1	B. & R. 83		3	B. 391
	2	Walker. 383	96	1	Ham. 135
79	1	C. 255		2	C. 267
	2	Tylden. G. *Society of Army Historical Research Journal.* 1957. 30		3	Cromb. 20
			97	1	Ham. 135
				2	C. 267
	3	N–N. 206		3	B. & R. 88
	4	N–N. 200	98	1	B. & R. 88
	5	Montgomery. 40		2	C. 270
	6	BBB. C.—2950		3	Ham. 135
80	1	B. & R. 84		4	BBB.
	2	N–N. 210		5	Bond. *History Today* XV, 7, 495
81	1	Cromb. 14			
	2	Ham. 131		6	Hendry. 137
	3	Vulliamy. 73	99	1	C. 270
82	1	Ham. 132	101	1	Tylden. 32
	2	B. & R. 84		2	Montgomery. 46
	3	C. 259		3	Montgomery. 44
	4	Bond, B. *History Today,* XV, 7, 493		4	Ham. 136
			102	1	Ham. 136
	5	*Huisgenoot,* Van der Walt, A. J. H., 27 Feb. 1943		2	B. & R. 89
				3	C. 272
				4	Cromb. 28
	6	BBB.	103	1	C. 273
83	1	C. 258		2	Napier. 101 (letter 7 March 1881)
	2	Ham. 134			
	3	Ham. 133		3	C. 273/4
	4	Ham. 139		4	C. 276
	5	B. 384		5	S–C
	6	Ham. 142		6	S–C
84	1	B. & R. 84	104	1	C. 276
85	1	C. 262		2	S–C
	2	Montgomery. 41		3	Haggard. 154
86	1	C. 259	105	1	B. 403
	2	Bond. 493		2	Ham. 137

REFERENCES

PAGE	REF. NO.	SOURCE	PAGE	REF. NO.	SOURCE
	3	Cromb. 25, 36		8	B. & R. 93
	4	Cromb. 29		9	C. 283
106	1	Cromb. 33	115	1	B. & R. 90
	2	N–N. 205		2	Cromb. 41
	3	B. & R. 90		3	C. 285
	4	N–N. 301		4	Ham. 137
	5	C. 307		5	C. 281
	6	B. 405		6	Cromb. 49/50
	7	B. 405		7	Cromb. 47
	8	B. 405		8	N–N. 205
107	1	S–C	116	1	BBB.
	2	Cromb. 36	117	1	N–N. 212
	3	C. 285		2	Private information
	4	B. 406	118	1	S–C
	5	N–N. 223		2	Cromb. 16
	6	Cromb. 36		3	Bond. 494
108	1	C. 285		1	B. 317
	2	Ham. 130	119	2	Montgomery. 46
109	1	N–N. 218		3	Report by Cmdt. Ferreira
	2	Report by Cmdt. Ferreira	121	1	Cromb. 53
110	1	C. 296	122	1	Montgomery. 36
	2	C. 297	125	1	Victoria. 198, 199
111	1	Cromb. 44		2	Trevelyan. 431
112	1	Marling. 543/4	126	1	N–N. 355
	2	S–C		2	Wood. 318, 319, Morley. 39
	3	Marling. 52–4	127	1	Garvin. 440
	4	B. & R. 82		2	Morley. 38
113	1	Montgomery. 46	128	1	Morley. 42
	2	C. 279	129	1	C. 329
114	1	S–C		2	Dellairs. 484.
	2	Montgomery. 47	131	1	C. 338
	3	C. 284		2	Wood. 324
	4	B. & R. 93.	137	1	Rudyard Kipling's Verse. Hodder & Stoughton, London, 1960, p. 242
	5	S–C			
	6	Ham. 143/4			
	7	Cromb. 41			

INDEX

INDEX

British Forces—*cont.*
of Foot (Northamptons), 38–
9, 46–9, 56–8, 73, 76–9, 86, 98,
112, 117, 119; 92nd Gordon
Highlanders, 65, 68–70, 72–3,
76–9, 81, 83, 85–6, 93, 96–8,
100, 103–5, 108, 109, 112–14,
118; 94th Foot (Connaught
Rangers), 26–9
British Policy, official, 7, 9–15, 18,
20, 21, 51, 53, 61, 63–4;
Federation scheme: *see* Federa-
tion
Bronkhorst Spruit, massacre at,
25–9, 36, 37, 41, 51, 55, 108
Buffalo River, 45, 83
Buller, General Sir Redvers, V.C.,
122
Bunker Hill, Battle of (1775), 1
Burgers, State-President Thomas
F., 10, 11, 13, 14, 18, 32
Butler, General Sir William, 71

Cambridge, H.R.H. Duke of, 41,
78
Cameron (war correspondent), 2,
78, 79, 115, 125
Cannons: *see* British Forces: Artil-
lery
Cape Colony, 6, 7, 10, 20, 31, 37,
129, 135
Cape of Good Hope, 5, 6
Cape Punishment Act (1836), 7
Cape Town, 5, 14, 52
Carnarvon, Fourth Earl of, 10–12,
15, 18, 33, 136
Carter, Thomas Fortescue, 2, 59,
66, 73, 75, 76n., 79, 83–4,
96–9, 102–4, 106–7, 113–15,
119n., 130–1
Cetewayo, King, 11, 13, 18, 19
Chaka, Zulu Chief, 11
Chamberlain, Rt. Hon. Joseph, 127
Chelmsford, General Lord, 18, 33,
72
China War (1860), 32
Civil war, threat of, 14
Coldstream, River, 42, 130
Colley, Major-General Sir George
Pomeroy, appointed High
Commissioner, 22; letters

from Lanyon, 24, 28; need to
take action, 29; character and
career, 31–5; situation con-
fronting, 36–8; advance
planned, 38–40; advance, 41;
ultimatum, 42; advance, 43;
reaches Mount Prospect, 44;
surveys terrain, 45; advance
to Laing's Nek 46–7; remarks
on failure, 50; reactions, 51–2;
plans revenge for defeat, 53–4;
advance, 55; counter-advance,
56–7; reconnaissance, 58;
reaches Mount Prospect, 59;
comments on progress of
campaign; reactions, 61–3;
at Newcastle, 64; correspond-
ence, 65–6; ultimatum to
Boers, 67; advance to Mount
Prospect, 68; to Laing's Nek,
69; reconnaissance of Majuba
Hill, 70–1; reasoning, 72;
military plans, 73–5; prepares
advance, 76; advance, 77–8;
strength of force, 78–9; advance; 80–1; at Majuba;
neglects to strengthen camp,
82–3; H.Q., 84; dispositions,
85; inactivity, 86, 88–93;
reconnaissance, 94; pessimism,
95; inactivity, 96; asleep, 97;
reviews situation, 99–100;
refuses bayonet charge, 101–2;
bewildered by British rout,
104; death; different reports,
105–7; burial, 108, 116; body
looted, 115; death reported in
London, 116; suicide theory,
117; dispositions discussed,
118–20; blamed for disaster,
120–2; aftermath, 125–36; survivors' history, 137–9, 140–2
Colley, Lady, 33, 47, 52, 54, 60,
64, 66, 72, 76, 106
Connaught Rangers: *see* British
Forces: 94th Foot
Constitution of South African
Republic, 8, 20
Crimean War (1853–56), 31
Cromb, David, 71
Cromwell, Oliver, 90

150

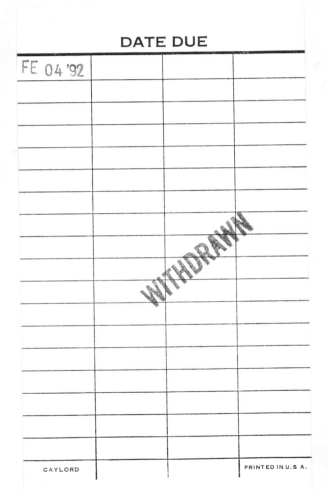